ALL ABOUT ANNUALS

Created and designed
by the editorial staff
of ORTHO Books

Written by
A. Cort Sinnes

Plant Selection Guide
Written by
Michael D. McKinley

Edited by
Ken Burke

Graphic design by
John Williams
Barbara Ziller

Front and back
cover photographs by
Kurt Reynolds

Publisher
Robert L. Iacopi

Editorial Director
Min S. Yee

Managing Editor
Anne Coolman

Horticultural Editor
Michael D. Smith

Senior Editor
Kenneth R. Burke

Production Manager
Laurie S. Blackman

Horticulturist
Michael McKinley

Associate Editors
Barbara J. Ferguson
Susan M. Lammers

Administrative Assistant
Judith C. Pillon

Production Assistant
Anne D. Pederson

Editorial Assistant
Julie W. Hall

Manuscript/Gardening Editor
Frank Shipe
San Francisco, California

Typography
Vera Allen Composition
Castro Valley, California

Color Separations
Balzer/Shopes
San Francisco, California

Address all inquiries to:
Ortho Books
Chevron Chemical Company
Consumer Products Division
575 Market Street
San Francisco, CA 94105

Printed in August, 1981.

1 2 3 4 5 6 7 8 9 10

ISBN 0-917102-91-6

Library of Congress Catalog Card
Number 80-85224

ACKNOWLEDGMENTS

Manuscript consultants

James W. Wilson,
Sycamore, Illinois

Professor Emeritus Joseph Lent,
Storrs, Connecticut

Marco Polo Stufano,
Wave Hill, Bronx, New York

Photo sources

Barry Ferguson, designer,
Oyster Bay, New York

Betty Rollins, Berkeley,
California

Boerner Gardens of Whitnall Park,
Hales Corner, Wisconsin

Cantigny Estate,
Wheaton, Illinois

Charles Wilson
of Joseph Harris Co., Inc.,
Rochester, New York

Denholm Seed Co., Inc.,
Gilroy, California

Dick Turner,
San Francisco, California

Dodge Freeman, designer,
Lake Forest, Illinois

Ferry Morse Seed Co., Inc.,
San Juan Bautista, California

Fred McGourty,
Brooklyn Botanic Garden,
Brooklyn, New York

Jack Romine,
Walnut Creek, California

Jane Gates, Helen Crocker Russell
Memorial Library of Strybing Arboretum
Society, Golden Gate Park,
San Francisco, California

Larry McDougald, nurseryman,
San Anselmo, California

Longwood Gardens,
Kennett Square, Pennsylvania

Mary Anne Ford of George J. Ball, Inc.,
West Chicago, Illinois

Marilyn Alimo, president,
The Garden Clubs of Illinois
Wave Hill, Bronx, New York

Niagara Parks Commission's
School of Horticulture,
Niagara Falls, Ontario, Canada

Sir John R. H. Thuron,
Unionville, Pennsylvania

The Bailey Arboretum,
Oyster Bay, New York

The Chicago Botanic Garden,
Chicago, Illinois

Photography

Names of photographers in
alphabetical order are followed
by page numbers on which their
work appears. R = right, C = center,
L = left, T = top, B = bottom.

William C. Aplin: 61C, 68R.

John Blaustein: 28, 31T, 42, 43,
44, 48B, 49B, 52, 54.

Josephine Coatsworth: 11, 13,
22, 23R, 27T, 34, 37R, 38,
46, 47R, 58C, 63L, 66R, 67R,
70L, 71R, 80, 84R, 88L,
88C, 90L, 92R.

Thomas E. Eltzroth: 76C.

Derek Fell: 5T, 60, 61L, 62L,
65T, 65R, 67C, 72R, 73, 74L,
76R, 77L, 78R, 81C, 82C, 83L,
86R, 88R.

David Fischer: 14, 16, 18, 20.

Michael Landis: 6T, 6 next-to-T,
6 next-to-B, 7, 9T, 25RT, 37T,
38, 47T, 48T, 49T, 59T, 59L,
66L, 66C, 69L, 71L, 76L, 77R,
82R, 84T, 84L, 85, 87, 89C, 93T.

Michael McKinley: Title page,
4, 6 next-to-B, 8, 23T, 25RB,
27B, 29B, 31B, 35, 36, 58L,
59R, 61R, 62R, 64T, 64R, 65L,
67L, 68L, 68C, 69C, 69R, 70C,
70R, 72L, 74R, 75, 77C, 78T,
78L, 81L, 83C, 86L, 86C, 89L,
90R, 91L, 91C, 91T.

James K. McNair: 5R, 9R, 12T, 50.

Colin C. McRae: 51.

Pan American Seed Co.: 58R,
63C, 68T.

Michael Smith: 89R.

Esta Stough: 82L.

Stylist

Sara Slavin: 14, 16, 18, 20, 28,
31T, 42, 43, 44, 48B, 49B, 52, 54

Flower arrangements

James McNair: 14, 16, 18, 20

Illustrator

Cindy Clark

Front cover: Viola cornuta 'Arkwright
Ruby'.

Back cover: A mixed border of petunias,
geraniums, marigolds, and violas.

Title page: Centaurea cyanus 'Snowball'.

ALL ABOUT ANNUALS

STAR PERFORMERS

For their yearly display of exuberant color, annuals certainly deserve to be called "star performers." Give them center stage and a little care, and they will steal any gardening show.

For most gardeners annuals mean flowers, and lots of them—in every conceivable shape, color, and size. There are many flowering plants for garden use, but as a group none is so willing to grow, easy to take care of, or inexpensive as annuals.

The word *annual* is common enough; yet when it is used to describe a group of garden plants, few people could give you an exact definition. The key to the definition is in the word itself: "annual" means yearly, and annual plants are those that complete their entire life cycle within one year or less. Their pattern of growth is illustrated each year in the garden: they are usually planted in the spring, flower through summer and fall, and die with the first frosts in winter. Annuals are temporary plants, as opposed to permanent plantings of trees, shrubs, vines, and ground covers, but their brief stay is a brilliant one, making them among the most popular of all plant choices.

OTHER FLOWERING PLANTS

Throughout this book are photographs of many gardens taken from around the country. As you become more familiar with which plants are annuals and which are not, you will notice that very few of the gardens pictured are composed entirely of annuals. If some of the flowering plants are not annuals, what are they?

The tree mallow is among the showiest of all annuals. The hibiscuslike flowers are nearly 3 inches across; the plants may grow to 3 feet.

Flowering plants (excluding the woody shrubs and trees) are generally broken into three groups according to their life cycles: *annuals, perennials,* and *biennials.* Annuals, as we have mentioned, are temporary plants that live out their lives within one year. In all but a few cases where they reseed themselves, new annuals must be planted each year.

Perennials, on the other hand, are more or less permanent plants in the garden. The stems and leaves may die back during the cold winter months, but the roots remain alive and send forth new and bigger plants each spring. If you are interested in knowing more about perennials, be sure and consult Ortho's *All About Perennials.*

The third classification—biennials—tends to confuse most gardeners. Biennials are plants that take two years, or two growth periods, to complete their life cycle: the first year they grow from seed into a leafy plant; the second year they flower, set seed, and die. What is confusing is that many biennials, such as foxglove, sweet William, and money plant, are usually purchased as started plants at the nursery. In effect, the grower has taken care of the first phase of the biennial's life, and the gardener sees only the second phase, in which the plant flowers and dies at the end of the growing season in the same fashion as the annuals.

Some perennials and biennials will, in favorable climates, come from seed to flower in a single growing season. These, then, may be treated as annuals, and for that reason are included in this book.

Forget-me-nots and rose-colored English daisies form a miniature version of an old-fashioned nosegay.

Hardy, Half-Hardy, and Tender

Throughout this book we will frequently refer to an annual as being hardy, half-hardy, or tender. These categories refer to the temperature ranges that various annuals need in order to germinate (sprout from seed) and grow successfully. They are good general guides as to the best times to plant the specific annuals and when to anticipate peak bloom.

The two most important dates to know, as they relate to the three categories, are the last frost in spring and the first frost in fall. Climate maps on the back of many seed packs will give an approximation of these dates. (For more detailed, localized information on your climate, talk to your County Extension Agent, nurseryman, or gardening neighbors; or keep your own records from year to year.)

Hardy annuals can stand the most cold of all, taking light frosts without being killed or badly damaged. In most cases, seeds of hardy annuals can be planted outdoors a couple of weeks before the last frost in spring, or after the soil begins to freeze in fall. Planted in fall they will lay dormant through the winter and then sprout in spring as soon as the soil begins to warm—alternating freezing and thawing will not hurt them. Remember that the word "hardy" applied to plants refers not to their general strength or vigor, but to the specific ability to withstand cold.

The seedlings or young plants of half-hardy annuals can tolerate long periods of damp or cold weather, but can be damaged or killed by frost. Seeds of most can be planted after the last possible frost in spring. Most kinds do not need soil temperatures as high as the tender annuals need to germinate, but some do require fairly warm soil. Seed packets or catalogs will point out the exceptions.

Tender annuals for the most part came originally from countries with the warmest climates. They need warm soil to germinate, and usually a fairly long warm summer to produce the best display of flowers. Do not plant seeds of tender annuals outdoors until the ground has thoroughly warmed; usually 2–3 weeks after the last frost in spring. If you live in a climate with a short growing season, it's best to buy tender annuals already started, or to start seeds indoors yourself, so that you have

seedlings ready to set out when the recommended planting time arrives. This will give you a good jump on the growing season and a better chance of producing plenty of flowers.

In addition to being vulnerable to cold, some tender annuals cannot withstand periods of extremely hot or humid weather. In the South and in low-elevation areas of the West, most "burn out" in midsummer. Successive plantings are necessary to sustain full color throughout the summer.

Reseeding

There are several flowering plants that reseed themselves freely at the end of the growing season. The seeds lie dormant during the winter, and start growing as soon as the soil warms to the proper temperature in spring. Alyssum, browallia, lobelia, ageratum, nicotiana, nasturtium, petunia, scabiosa, cleome, foxglove, and hollyhock are just some that readily reseed.

The degree to which a plant reseeds itself is determined by several factors: the variety of the plant, the type of seed it produces, and the climate in which you garden. Plants closest to the original species (as it was collected from the wild) are far more likely to reseed and produce plants similar to their parents than are those that resulted from extensive hybridization by plant breeders. Seeds of some species are remarkably tolerant of a wide range of germinating conditions and are naturally very fertile; these are far more likely to germinate year after year than those with specific cultural and climatic germination needs.

Many gardeners tend to regard seedlings that pop up unexpectedly in their flower beds as a bonus from last year's crop. Sometimes they are, but this is not always so; plants out of place can be nuisance weeds. Chance, or "volunteer," seedlings of hybrid types also can revert to poor quality flowers with muddy colors.

Where winters are long and cold, only the hardiest species will reseed themselves and survive. In mild-winter regions of the South and West, however, successful reseeding is a common occurrence. And in areas with frost-free winters, some annuals may not die at all. Gardeners in these benign climates often treat the cold-tolerant annuals almost like perennials: cut back severely in fall and allowed to rest during the mild winter, by spring they're ready to grow again, often rewarding the gardener with displays of extra-early flowers.

Examples of hardy, half-hardy, and tender annuals (from top to bottom): Iceland poppy, gazania, and nicotiana, Left: California poppies are among the annuals that reseed themselves readily each year.

NAMED VARIETIES

Throughout this book we will often refer to named varieties of a particular annual. Beginning gardeners are often content with simply the name of the annual, such as marigold or petunia. But as you garden from one year to the next, you'll soon find that one named variety outperforms another, and from that point on you'll be on a "first-name basis" with several members of a particular group of annuals, asking for 'Royal Blue' alyssum or 'Queen of Hearts' dianthus, for example, instead of simply dianthus or alyssum.

Botanically speaking, there are two different groups of varieties: those that occur naturally in the wild are called "horticultural varieties," and those that are produced under controlled conditions by plant breeders are known as "cultivated varieties" (frequently combined and shortened to *cultivars*). However, this technical distinction matters little to the home gardener, whose main concern is to become familiar enough with all the available varieties to know which ones will grow best in his or her own garden. As you are probably already aware, there are thousands of named varieties of annuals. An organization known as the All-America Selections does some of the experimenting and comparing for you, making the job of choosing one named variety over another a little easier.

You probably have run across the words "All-America Selections" while reading a seed catalog, or on a trip to the garden center. What do they mean?

All-America Selections is an organization composed of a council of judges and some 50 official test gardens across the United States and Canada. The purpose of these gardens and judges is the yearly evaluation of new vegetable and flower varieties introduced by seed companies the world over, by universities, and by private individuals.

Trial rows of the All-America entries are grown in side-by-side comparison with the most similar varieties already in commerce. To ensure impartiality, the new entries are known to the judges by number only.

From the 75 to 100 vegetable and flower entries made in an average year, only 3 or 4 may be voted enough points to earn All-America medals, but in other years as many as 8 awards have been made. Judges try to place themselves in the shoes of the home gardener, and vote primarily on home-gardening merit. However, a flower variety should also be a reliable producer of seeds, and if possible, adaptable to

starting in packs or pots for sale as growing plants.

The judges also pay special attention to each entry's climatic adaptation, vigor, and length of bloom season. With test gardens in the different climates of the United States and Canada, the home gardener can be sure an All-America Selection is not only the best in its class, but is also adapted to a wide range of soils, climates, and cultural practices.

HOW TO USE THIS BOOK

This book is both an idea book and a handbook of basic information. It contains ideas for planting and using annuals in a variety of new and imaginative ways, and explores some of the time-honored principles of color, aesthetics, and garden design. But perhaps even more importantly, it contains all the practical information you need in order to produce a beautiful flower garden.

If you've never planted annuals in a big way before, you'll benefit by reading *Gardening with Color*, starting on page 9. The most outstanding characteristic of annuals is the wide range of colors they bring to the garden—so many, in fact, that the beginning gardener may be somewhat unsure of what colors and combinations to plant. This section offers sound advice on color and how to make it work for you.

If you are planning a new garden emphasizing flowering plants, be sure and read *Annuals in the Landscape*, beginning on page 23. Here you'll find valuable information on garden design, choosing plants, and complementing your home with the beauty of container and cut flowers.

If you're interested in growing annuals from seed to save money and get flowers early, *Starting Annuals from Seed*, page 37, will give you detailed instructions in the most successful methods you can use.

For virtually everything you need to know to grow healthy, vigorous flowering annuals, see *From the Ground Up*, page 47.

And finally, for a quick and handy reference to the annuals, the *Plant Selection Guide*, beginning on page 57, contains photographs and descriptions of more than 100 plants. Each entry contains the "hard facts" on colors and sizes available, cultural requirements, and possible uses to the gardener. It also offers more detailed information on problem areas and how to get the best health and bloom from each plant.

Most annuals have a specific name given to them by a plant breeder or seed company. Named varieties make it easier for gardeners to distinguish one variety from another from one year to the next. Top: Zinnia 'Cherry Ruffle.' Bottom: Dianthus 'Snow Fire.'

GARDENING WITH COLOR

Name any color, and nine times out of ten you will find an annual flower to match it. With a little knowledge of the principles of color and a willingness to experiment, gardeners can create any combination or effect they desire.

When you walk for the first time into a garden filled with flowering plants, the memory you will most likely take home with you is of the colors, rather than the flower forms, the garden design, or some other feature. It's true that a successful garden is made up of more than just color, but color is the most impressive and memorable of all garden qualities.

In the gardener's dictionary, the word "annual" is practically synonymous with the word "color." Annual flowering plants are the fastest, least expensive, most satisfying way to achieve quantities of garden color. Perhaps most impressive of all is that almost every color, shade, and tint is available in one flower or another.

On the next few pages we'll discuss some of the time-honored principles as they apply to color in the garden, principles that designers and artists have employed for centuries. The value of these principles has been proven over time, but color is a highly personal subject, and the garden is a forgiving place, where even "mistakes" can have merit. All gardeners should have the opportunity to discover on their own what rules apply to their own gardens and tastes.

The fact that annuals are not permanent plants gives the gardener considerable flexibility: if you discover that you don't like a certain combination of colors, the arrangement can be modified the next year. Unlike the

Sometimes no color scheme is the best scheme of all. Shown here is a combination of rose, violet, and lavender phlox, yellow and deep purple pansies, and orange marigolds.

more or less permanent members of your garden, annuals are primarily warm-season visitors. Because of the annuals' transitory nature, many adventurous gardeners feel free to completely change their annual color scheme from one year to the next.

Gardening with color is an activity as exciting as any other creative endeavor, with the added excitement that comes from working with living, changing materials. Ideas for color schemes can come from anywhere: a neighbor's garden, the colors found in a single blossom, or from something as practical as new exterior paint on your house. With every planting of annuals you'll learn more about what color or combinations you like best, which plants are the most vigorous growers, or which varieties you wouldn't plant again. Gardening with annual color is a continual process of discovery, with the potential for new rewards each season.

The color wheel shown here may remind you of an art class, but don't be put off by its formal appearance: a color wheel is simply the easiest way to explain the basic interrelationships among colors.

The wheel is often used to point out the three primary colors—red, yellow, and blue—and to show how the other colors on the wheel are made from blending various quantities of these three. Because one can't blend or mix two colors of flowers to produce a third, this information is more important to artists than to gardeners. What is important to gardeners, however, is how colors clash with or complement one another, and the distinction between "warm" and "cool" colors.

A combination of orange-red wallflower and turquoise blue forget-me-nots makes a dazzling combination in this border planting. For the talented gardener almost any combination of colors is possible with annual flowers.

A little knowledge of color can help gardeners produce results as pleasing as the border shown below. Warm-colored flowers were favored: scarlet zinnias gold celosia, and yellow marigolds. The light-yellow marigolds draw attention to the rear of the border, making it seem closer to the viewer.

COLOR WHEEL

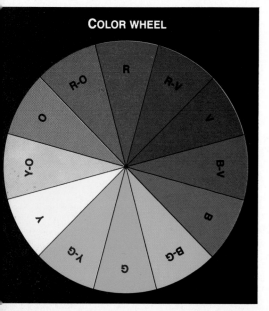

WARM AND COOL COLORS

The colors in the wheel can be divided into warm and cool colors. Colors, of course, are neither physically warm nor cool; but they can make you *feel* either way. The colors on the left-side of the wheel, from yellow to red, are considered the warm colors. Those colors on the right-hand side, from green to violet, are cool colors. Red-violet and yellow-green have both warm and cool properties, one more than the other depending on what other colors they are combined with.

The distinction between warm and cool colors is important to the gardener for several reasons. For instance, if you have a light- or warm-colored house with a patio or deck on the southern side, you may already have a problem with too much heat. Planting warm-colored annuals in and around this area will make it seem even warmer. However, if you plant with plenty of cool green, blue, violet, and pastel colors, the area won't actually be any cooler, but it will seem so and be a more inviting place.

Another important consideration is that to the eye, cool colors tend to recede, and warm colors to advance.

In practice, this means that cool-colored flowers at the far end of the garden tend to disappear, but warm colors will be quite noticeable.

Be conscious, too, of how you combine warm and cool colors. For example, if you had a garden composed primarily of cool-colored flowers, a mass of flame orange zinnias in the background would divert attention from the more subtle colors in the foreground, and disrupt the harmonious effect.

Generally speaking, cool colors are good for close-up viewing and warm colors are good for dramatic displays. The cool colors of dark blue lobelia, purple petunias, or blue salvia, for instance, may make quite an impact next to the patio or walkway, but planted in the background of the garden they would all but lose their effect, especially if the area were shaded.

Knowing that the warm colors stand out and shout, you can bring a distant part of the yard into sharp focus with a planting of yellow or gold marigolds, any of the members of the sunflower family, cosmos 'Diablo', or some other sunny-colored annual.

COLOR SCHEMES

In certain combinations, colors have a harmonious effect. These harmonies are frequently discussed in four categories, easily identified on the color wheel.

Monochromatic color schemes involve the various tints and shades of one, and one only, of the pure colors (often called a *hue*) on the wheel. A *tint* is lighter than the pure color, and a *shade* is darker. Many of the most impressive flower gardens are planted in a monochromatic color scheme. An example would be red, various tints of pink, and a deep shade of red or maroon. Think of a combination of maroon snapdragons, red and rose-colored nicotiana, and pale pink dianthus, and you can begin to see the possibilities of such a color scheme. In reality, there are no totally monochromatic flower gardens: the various shades of "leaf green" will always be part of the combination; but their presence is a pleasant one that does not detract from the more predominant flower colors.

Many people take the monochromatic color scheme a step further, and plan a display of flowers to complement the color of the house. This "total color concept" can be particularly effective and is worth experimenting with.

Analogous color schemes make use of "neighbors" on the color wheel; any three colors used in the same sequence in which they are found on the color wheel are said to comprise an analogous relationship. An example would be: red-violet, violet, and blue-violet.

You expand the possibilities of such a color scheme when you include the tints and shades of each of the colors. Because you have more flowers and colors to choose from, an analogous color scheme is easier to work with than a strictly monochromatic one, and the results can be truly memorable.

Gertrude Jekyll (1843–1932), an English writer and gardener *extraordinaire* whose influence helped produce some of the world's greatest gardens, developed what she called a "tonal" garden, based on rules similar to those for an analogous color scheme.

In the best of these gardens planned by Jekyll (there are several still in existence), all of the colors, including leaf color, are tonally related. One garden (Folly Farm in Berkshire, England) planted at the turn of the century made use of silver-leafed plants and white, pale lavender, and ivory flowers. The colors of the foliage and flowers, in turn, complemented the colors of the stone walks and walls.

Top: A subtle monochromatic combination of forget-me-knots and 'Imperial Blue' pansies. The minute details on each flower invite close-up inspection. Above: In this commercial flower field, orange, red, and red-violet zinnias graphically show why analogous color schemes are favorites of many gardeners.

Top: Not many gardeners take advantage of the unusual effect of a complementary color scheme. Shown in this bed are blue forget-me-nots and golden yellow wallflowers. Part of the appeal in this particular combination is the even texture of the finely cut foliage and small flowers. Above: The pastel colors of spring are echoed in this planting of yellow and lavender violas, white candytuft, and a variety of daffodils.

If this type of tonally related garden appeals to you, the following are suggestions for gray- or silver-foliaged plants: dusty miller 'Silver Queen', gray santolina, 'Tricolor' sage, snow-in-summer, artemisia 'Silver Queen', 'White Christmas' caladiums, lavender, and many members of the dianthus family. Some of the best white-flowering annuals include: ageratum, asters, petunias, morning glory, verbena, and lobelia.

Complementary colors appear directly opposite one another on the color wheel. These are powerful combinations: red and green, orange and blue, yellow and violet, and so on. For the maximum effect, flowers of the purest hues (rather than shades or tints) should be combined: a few possibilities are orange 'Pumpkin Crush' marigolds and blue cornflowers, bright yellow nasturtiums and violet 'Amethyst' verbena, scarlet red 'Comanche' petunias or 'Toreador' celosia combined with nothing but their own green leaves or other foliage plants.

Some people might say these colors clash, others might find them vibrant and vital. Often, complementary combinations of very strong colors are predominantly displayed in parks and other public areas. For

most people's tastes they are not the best choices for the small garden. Confining a powerful color scheme in a small space intensifies its effect and can make it overwhelming.

If you want to try to "blend" strong complementary colors, place the plants so they intermingle where they meet, rather than keeping them separate with a more or less straight line. Intermingling colors in this way enhances their vibrancy, and from a distance they will appear to blend somewhat at the edges. If you wish to tone them down, include groups of the silvery-leafed or white-flowered annuals.

Polychromatic color schemes can produce a carnival-like effect in the garden. The random coupling of any—and every—color around the wheel is often the result of the gardener's inexperience. There is nothing wrong with this type of color scheme; indeed, there are many who go so far as to claim that because there are no "mistakes" in nature's own color scheme, it's also impossible for the gardener to produce one. One benefit of random plantings is the possibility of "happy accidents"—color combinations that may become the mainstay of the garden for seasons to come.

Experimenting with Color

If you are reluctant to combine certain flower colors, one good way to experiment on a small scale is to plant combinations in pots or other containers. Or, plant one kind in each pot and move the pots about until you find combinations that please you. This does not require much time or effort, and the results can be surprisingly good. The plantings can then be carried out on a larger scale in the garden.

The great English gardener Vita Sackville-West used to carry a branch of a flowering plant or shrub around the garden until she found a place where it was most pleasing. It was then, and only then, that she either decided to leave the plant where it was or move it to a new, more desirable location.

You can do the same thing with several pots of experimental color combinations, trying them in front of the house, the back, next to the steps, or wherever, until you find a spot where they look best with the plants already growing there.

For more about gardening with color, using all types of plants, see Ortho's *Gardening with Color*.

A Color Sampler

In the next eight pages we present a sampling of flowers, grouped according to color. The bouquets, gathered in the height of summer, are representative, but by no means all-inclusive, of the annual flowers you can grow in your own garden.

Each of the four photographs shows an assortment of flowers loosely grouped around one of the three primary colors of red, yellow, and blue. Because of their popularity and importance in the garden, we have also included a collection of white and cream-colored flowers. These photographs not only show you specific examples of various flowers and colors, but will also give you an idea of the different flower forms to choose from. On the page facing each of the photographs you will find a list of the best flowers to choose from in that particular color group.

The carnival-confetti look of a polychromatic flower border can be intentional or accidental. Either way, the results can be fresh and lighthearted. Among the flowers shown here (from front to back) are orange, red, and hot-pink zinnias, yellow snapdragons, pink, lavender, and white china asters, gold marigolds, and pink and white cosmos.

RED

Red is quite a color. It is a little like the distant relative who always seems to shake things up at annual family gatherings—the color red has that same power. True reds are compelling. They invite closer inspection. They tempt. They are big colors and can be overwhelming for people with less adventurous tastes.

There was a time when attitudes toward color were arbitrary and strictly dictated. We found the following advice in the 1946 edition of *The New Garden Encyclopedia* and, as amusing as it now sounds, we wondered whether or not it contained an element of truth: "Red flowers are favorable for the weak and ailing to sit among, for rapid growing children below the physical norm to play in the midst of, for the aged and feeble to dwell with. We gather that it is an unfavorable color for general use, however, because of the tendency of workers under red light to irritability and quarrelsomeness; not until they were removed from it or allowed to spend part of their time in the blue room did they become normal."

With those admonitions aside, there are several garden designers who think that a garden really isn't complete without at least some red in it. And it's undeniable that a little red here and there really does spark other colors into life. Treat red with respect and it will treat your garden to a little excitement.

Flowers in a pure red hue are rare. Look for 'Scarlet Flash' geraniums, 'Comanche' petunias, 'Red Hussar' salvia, 'Idol' and red 'Nicki' nicotiana, 'Blaze' verbena, the scarlet red 'Ruffles' and 'Red Sun' zinnias, and amaranthus 'Illumination'.

In mixing pigments, when the pure color red is softened with white it becomes another creature altogether. If red stands for force and vigor, pink stands for quite the opposite. The color is usually associated with diminutive flowers that require close-up inspection. And because of the number of fragrant pink flowers, like dianthus, petunias, sweet peas, and stock, most people think of pink as a sweet-smelling color.

A classic but seldom-used combination is pink and red—especially effective in the garden, where the green foliage adds a moderating touch. Planted against a white wall or fence, the combination looks particularly fresh. Red petunias and pink verbena, red and pink geraniums together in the same container, or tall pink snapdragons and red salvia are just a few possibilities.

ANNUALS WITH RED TO PINK FLOWERS

Amaranthus species (Jacob's Coat; Love-Lies-Bleeding)
Alcea rosea (Hollyhock)
Antirrhinum majus (Snapdragon)
Begonia × semperflorens-cultorum (Wax-leaf Begonia)
Callistephus chinensis (China Aster)
Capsicum annuum (Ornamental Pepper)
Cataranthus roseus (Madagascar Periwinkle)
Celosia cristata (Cockscomb)
Clarkia hybrids (Godetia; Farewell-to-Spring)
Cleome hasslerana (Spider Flower)
Coleus × hybridus (Coleus)
Consolida ambigua (Rocket Larkspur)
Cosmos bipinnatus (Mexican Aster)
Cuphea ignea (Mexican Cigar Plant)
Dahlia hybrids (Dahlia)
Dianthus species (China Pink; Sweet William)
Dimorphotheca sinuata (Cape Marigold)
Eschscholzia californica (California Poppy)
Gaillardia pulchella (Blanket Flower)
Gazania rigens (Gazania)
Gerbera jamesonii (Transvaal Daisy)
Gypsophila elegans (Annual Baby's Breath)
Helichrysum bracteatum (Strawflower)
Iberis species (Candytuft)
Impatiens species (Balsam; Impatiens)
Ipomea × multifida (Cardinal Climber)
Ipomea quamoclit (Cypress Vine)
Lathyrus odorata (Sweet Pea)
Lavatera hybrids (Tree Mallow)
Linaria maroccana (Toadflax)
Matthiola incana (Stock)
Mimulus × hybridus (Monkey Flower)
Nemesia strumosa (Pouch Nemesia)
Nicotiana alba (Flowering Tobacco)
Nigella damascena (Love-in-a-Mist)
Papaver species (Poppy)
Pelargonium × hortorum (Geranium)
Phlox drummondii (Annual Phlox)
Petunia × hybrida (Petunia)
Portulaca grandiflora (Rose Moss)
Rhynchelytrum roseum (Ruby Grass)
Salpiglossis sinuata (Painted Tongue)
Salvia splendens (Scarlet Sage)
Scabiosa atropurpurea (Pincushion Flower)
Schizanthus × wisetonensis (Poor Man's Orchid)
Tropaeolum majus (Nasturtium)
Verbena × hybrida (Garden Verbena)
Viola × wittrockiana (Pansy)
Zinnia elegans (Zinnia)

Included in the bouquets at left are (from top to bottom): dianthus, zinnias, cosmos, nicotiana, asters, salpiglossis, scabiosa, celosia, and snapdragons.

Blue

For some gardeners, blue flowers are like an addiction. As sought after as they are, there aren't many truly blue flowers, and the process of collecting them and planting them in one place can become a lifelong passion. An all-blue garden demands a viewer's full attention, not only because of the rarity of the colors, but also to appreciate the jewel-like quality of many of the flowers.

When you expand the color spectrum a bit to include the shades and tints of purple and violet, you can create combinations with the rich intensity of a stained glass window. Consider that the deep shades of these colors are often difficult to distinguish from the foliage, especially if the plants are in a shady location. Plant flowers in these colors in a bright location close to the house where they can be easily admired. The addition of white or pink flowers will also help add vibrancy.

The family of blue includes many richly colored flowers. Some of the more intense colors can be achieved with the following varieties: 'Amethyst' and 'Sparkle' verbena, 'Violet Flame' salvia, 'Sapphire' lobelia, 'Sugar Daddy', 'Blue Mariner' and 'Malibu' petunias, azure blue asters, and 'Blue Boy' cornflowers.

The out-of-print *New Garden Encyclopedia*, which we quoted on the subject of the color red, had an equally unreserved opinion of the blues. The editor suggests "a blue garden for the nervous and highly-strung, for the tired business man, for the child given to violent outbursts. Being the antithesis of red, blue is not a stimulating color and should be kept out of a garden if sluggish temperaments are in need of stirring and awakening. But it may prove of great help to the student or any desirous of contemplative retreat."

If the deeper shades of blue, violet, and purple tend to recede into the overall garden, their best qualities are highlighted when combined for an indoor bouquet, as you can see in the picture at left. For this reason alone, flowers in this color range are worth planting. If they don't fit into your regular garden color scheme, consider planting them in a separate cutting garden (see page 31).

Many gardeners give these colors the sharper focus they need by planting them in containers and placing them in conspicuous places. Planted with a combination of powder blue ageratum, purple zinnias, dark blue lobelia, and 'Malibu' petunias, a few containers clustered around a deck or patio serve as living outdoor bouquets.

Seed companies are well aware of the optical effects of dark flowers. In color mixtures of seeds they include only a few of the dark shades, a like amount of white, and make up the bulk of the seed from pastel and bright colors.

ANNUALS WITH BLUE, VIOLET, AND PURPLE FLOWERS

Ageratum houstanianum (Floss Flower)
Anchusa capensis (Cape Forget-Me-Not)
Browallia speciosa (Sapphire Flower)
Callistephus chinensis (China Aster)
Campanula medium (Canterbury Bells)
Centauria cyanus (Bachelor Button)
Consolida ambigua (Rocket Larkspur)
Convolvulus tricolor (Dwarf Morning Glory)
Cynoglossum amabile (Chinese Forget-Me-Not)
Gomphrena globosa (Globe Amaranth)
Heliotropium arborescens (Heliotrope)
Ipomea leptophylla (Bush Morning Glory)
Ipomea nil; I. purpurea; I. tricolor (Morning Glory)
Lathyrus odorata (Sweet Pea)
Limonium sinuatum (Notch-leaf Sea Lavender)
Lobelia erinus (Edging Lobelia)
Myosotis sylvatica (Forget-Me-Not)
Nemophila menziesii (Baby Blue Eyes)
Nigella damascena (Love-in-a-Mist)
Nierembergia hippomanica (Cup Flower)
Petunia × hybrida (Petunia)
Salpiglossis sinuata (Painted Tongue)
Salvia splendens (Scarlet Sage)
Salvia farinacea (Blue Sage)
Scabiosa atropurpurea (Pincushion Flower)
Torenia fourneri (Wishbone Flower)
Trachymene coerulea (Blue Lace Flower)
Verbena × hybrida (Garden Verbena)
Viola × wittrockiana (Pansy)

Flowers in the blue violet range of the spectrum include (from top to bottom): bachelor's buttons, nigella, lobelia, campanula, cosmos, statice, scabiosa, foxglove, asters, and celosia.

WHITE

White flowers are special to many gardeners. In fact, there have been many famous gardens given over to white flowering plants alone. The color white suggests purity—a quality most people admire in gardens.

White reflects the most light of any color. Even at night, when other colors in the garden are subdued by darkness, white flowers shimmer in whatever light is available; the effect in moonlight can be spellbinding. White flowers are a powerful element in the garden and should be used wherever you want sparkle and light.

White flowers are also the favorites of many designers who find special appeal in the graphic contrast of masses of white flowers against lush, dark green foliage plants. Add a few white garden chairs, a small brick patio, and a black and white striped awning, and you've got a million dollar look. Pure white annuals include: 'White Cascade' petunias, several varieties of stock, 'Purity' cosmos, white 'Carefree' and 'Sprinter' geraniums, 'Snow Carpet' ageratum, 'Carpet of Snow' alyssum, and 'Snowflake' dianthus.

Cream and ivory-colored flowers lack the brightness of pure white but possess a rich quality all their own. Cream-colored flowers are not remarkable for their ability to combine well with other colors (except yellow), but by themselves—particularly in cut flower arrangements—they are extremely attractive. Among the best annuals in ivory shades are: 'Carved Ivory' zinnias, 'Cream Puff' marigolds, 'Italian White' sunflowers, and white 'Rocket' snapdragons.

Flowers in these white and cream arrangements include (from top to bottom): nigella, mignonette, phlox, baby's breath, cosmos, petunias, bells of Ireland, zinnias, and stock.

ANNUALS WITH CREAM TO WHITE FLOWERS

Ageratum houstanianum (Floss Flower)
Alcea rosea (Hollyhock)
Antirrhinum majus (Snapdragon)
Arctotis stoechadifolia var. *grandis* (African Daisy)
Begonia × *semperflorens-cultorum* (Waxleaf Begonia)
Callistephus chinensis (China Aster)
Cataranthus roseus (Madagascar Periwinkle)
Cleome hasslerana (Spider Flower)
Dahlia Hybrids (Dahlia)
Dianthus species (China Pink; Sweet William)
Dimorphotheca sinuata (Cape Marigold)
Eschscholzia californica (California Poppy)
Gerbera Jamesonii (Transvaal Daisy)
Gypsophila elegans (Annual Baby's Breath)
Helichrysum bracteatum (Strawflower)
Iberis species (Candytuft)
Impatiens balsamina (Balsam)
Impatiens wallerana (Busy Lizzie; Impatiens)
Ipomea alba (Moonflower Vine)
Lathyrus odorata (Sweet Pea)
Lobelia erinus (Edging Lobelia)
Lobularia maritima (Sweet Alyssum)
Matthiola incana (Stock)
Nicotiana alba (Flowering Tobacco)
Papaver species (Poppy)
Pelargonium × *hortorum* (Geranium)
Phlox drummondii (Annual Phlox)
Petunia × *hybrida* (Petunia)
Salvia splendens (Scarlet Sage)
Scabiosa atropurpurea (Pincushion Flower)
Thunbergia alata (Black-eyed Susan Vine)
Verbena × *hybrida* (Garden Verbena)
Viola × *wittrockiana* (Pansy)

YELLOW

Perhaps it is because yellow is the color of the sun, the color associated with light and happiness, that it so frequently appears in gardens. Masses of yellow flowers bring an exuberant, cheerful quality to any garden. Its very presence seems to reaffirm the positive nature of gardening.

There is nothing quite so vibrant as a border of golden yellow nasturtiums next to a spring green lawn, as warm as a full marigold blossom in the peak of summer, or as faintly nostalgic as a planting of yellow and mahogany-colored snapdragons beside a rain-soaked garden path. Yellow is a powerful color, capable of evoking many moods.

To enhance the lively effects of yellow, try combining it with white; the effect practically sparkles. Try white ageratum with 'Sunburst' petunias, white zinnias with 'Lemon Drop' marigolds, or yellow 'Pacific Beauty' calendulas with white 'Carpet of Snow' alyssum.

When yellow is combined with pale blue, the result is fresh and cheerful. 'Powderpuff' ageratum and 'First Lady' marigolds, 'Blue Cascade' or 'Cambridge Blue' lobelia, and yellow calceolaria are all reliable choices.

Yellow infused with red or brown produces the gold, orange, and red-orange spectrum. There are many flowers in these shades, most often appearing in the height of summer or in early fall. Planted together they can mirror the colorful change of the seasons from summer to fall. They don't command attention like pure red or yellow, but this is all to the better for many people's tastes. Flowers in these colors include: the annual chrysanthemums 'Rainbow' and 'Golden Raindrops', 'Lollipop' gaillardias, 'Sunshine' gazanias, strawflowers, single rudbeckia in russet shades, 'Black-eyed Susan' vine (*Thunbergia alata*), and the 'Old Mexico' zinnias.

Among the flowers in the yellow-to-orange range of the spectrum are (from top to bottom): marigolds, nasturtiums, strawflowers, calendula, cosmos, gaillardia, celosia, zinnias, sunflowers, and snapdragons.

ANNUALS WITH YELLOW, ORANGE, AND BRONZE FLOWERS

Alcea rosea (Hollyhock)
Antirrhinum majus (Snapdragon)
Calendula officinalis (Pot Marigold)
Celosia cristata (Cockscomb)
Coreopsis tinctoria (Calliopsis)
Cosmos sulphureus (Orange Cosmos)
Dahlia hybrids (Dahlia)
Dimorphotheca sinuata (Cape Marigold)
Dyssodia tenuiloba (Dahlberg Daisy)
Eschscholzia californica (California Poppy)
Gaillardia pulchella (Blanket Flower)
Gazania rigens (Gazania)
Gerbera jamesonii (Transvaal Daisy)
Gomphrena globosa (Glove Amaranth)
Helianthus species (Sunflower)
Impatiens balsamina (Balsam)
Lathyrus odorata (Sweet Pea)
Limonium bonduellii (Algerian Sea Lavender)
Linaria maroccana (Toadflax)
Matthiola incana (Stock)
Mimulus × hybridus (Monkey Flower)
Nemesia strumosa (Pouch Nemesia)
Papaver species (Poppy)
Pelargonium × hortorum (Geranium)
Portulaca grandiflora (Rose Moss)
Rudbeckia hirta var. *pulcherrima* 'Gloriosa Daisy' (Gloriosa Daisy)
Sanvitalia procumbens (Creeping Zinnia)
Tagetes species (Marigolds)
Thunbergia alata (Black-eyed Susan Vine)
Tithonia rotundifolia (Mexican Sunflower)
Tropaeolum majus (Nasturtium)
Verbena × hybrida (Garden Verbena)
Viola × wittrockiana (Pansy)
Zinnia species (Zinnia)

ANNUALS IN THE LANDSCAPE

Any successful garden is built on more than meets the eye. Good design, balanced proportion, and the many planting possibilities available should be considered before the first annual plant is put in the ground.

Because annuals are relatively small in size, easy to grow, inexpensive, and temporary, they have a rightful place in almost any part of the home landscape. This chapter tells you in easy steps how to design your own flower garden. It takes a look at the traditional use of annuals in beds and borders and as quick-growing, temporary screens and fill-in plants. It presents some popular ways to use annuals in containers and hanging baskets, indoors and out, and tells you how to plant and care for them as container plants. We will also take a look at the old-fashioned cutting garden as a modern source of flowers for indoor use.

DESIGNING A FLOWER GARDEN

If all flower gardens have one thing in common, namely beautiful flowering plants, what is it that makes one garden more attractive than another? In almost every case, the best are those with a strong underlying design or structure.

At some point in any successful garden's beginning, a thoughtful plan was devised and carried out on the landscape. The shape and size of the lawn, the paths and walkways, decks, patios, and other sitting areas, shade trees, shrub borders, hedges, ponds, and statues all were considered both individually and in light of how each contributed to create a total scene.

A casual combination of willowy dark pink cosmos and salmon pink petunias add an inviting touch to this narrow space in an entryway garden.

Unfortunately this planning stage is one often ignored by beginning gardeners: the majority of our gardens grow willy-nilly by bits and pieces, and if some overall design eventually does emerge, it is more by luck than by conscious effort. Most gardeners are faced with one of two situations: renovating an existing garden planted by a former owner; or creating a new garden from bare earth surrounding a new home. In either case the temptation is to hurry off to the nursery or garden center to buy a few plants for immediate results. In the long run, however, you will create a more beautiful garden if you take the extra time to draw some type of overall plan.

By the time your garden matures, the underlying structure or design may not be as apparent as when the plants were still young, but the organization it gives the garden will still be strongly felt. The sense of order a plan provides is important, particularly in flower gardens. With a variety of flowering plants of different sizes, shapes, colors, and forms, there is always the possibility of ending up with a jumble, or a jungle-like scene. But if the "bones" of the garden are strong, any combination of plants and flowers can be supported easily, without the fear of chaos taking control.

Beds and borders have been the key element in garden design as long as there have been gardens. What are they, and how do they differ? Simply put, a bed is a cultivated area surrounded by an open expanse, usually a grass lawn. A bed is accessible from all sides. A border, on the

A small patch of brightly colored dahlias and marigolds enlivens the starkness of white plaster walls and pleases all who pass by this wrought-iron gate.

A TYPICAL FORMAL GARDEN PLAN

A TYPICAL INFORMAL GARDEN PLAN

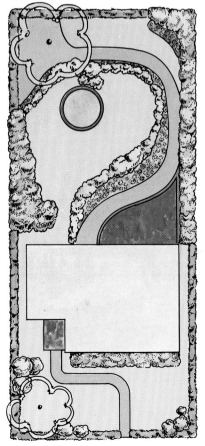

other hand, is at the edge of an area, lying next to a fence or walkway, or ringing the perimeter of a lawn. In most cases a border is accessible from the front side only.

Garden design basically calls for four steps:

▶Determining the point from which the garden will most often be seen.
▶Considering the shape and topography of your yard and which plants are there that are immovable or that you want to keep.
▶Deciding whether you want a formal or informal design.
▶Deciding whether you want beds or borders, or both.

The first step in planning a flower garden should be to determine from what angle or location the scene will be most often viewed. Planting a flower garden is much like painting a picture: in both instances the "artist" uses color to create something pleasant and interesting to look at. If the garden will be viewed primarily from inside the house, make sure the picture through your favorite window is the one you want to see. If you spend a lot of time on a deck or patio, you'll make it even more enjoyable by laying out your garden with that spot in mind.

Once you determine the angle from which your garden will be most often enjoyed, the next decision is one of style: will you lay out the garden on formal, straight lines, or on a less formal, naturalistic design of random curves?

Formal/informal. The decision to plan a formal or informal garden may be influenced as much by the existing conditions of your lot as by your aesthetic preferences. If the topography of your yard is irregular, with slopes, hills, or rock outcroppings, or if there are a number of mature trees that you wish to leave standing, you'll find it difficult to carry out a formal design. Such a site lends itself naturally to an informal plan, and most gardeners with these conditions will be content to let them dictate the style. On the other hand, if your yard is relatively flat, with no outstanding natural features, you'll be free to choose whatever style you wish.

Formal gardens are composed primarily of straight lines and classical symmetry—that is, what appears on the right side of the garden is matched, sometimes nearly perfectly, to the left side. The outermost dimension of the garden is frequently rectangular, and this shape is repeated in other parts of the plan—in pools, patios, and flower beds and borders. Often a single object, such as a statue, pool, or sundial, is chosen as the center of interest; for optimum effect, it is usually placed toward the rear of the garden, directly in the line of sight from your favorite viewing spot. A formal design is the easiest type of garden to lay out, and, because of its visual simplicity, is the best choice for a small lot.

In an informal garden there is a predominance of curved flowing lines and a seeming disregard for symmetry. The curves of lawn areas, patios, walkways, beds, and borders are usually gentle, wide arcs that frequently follow the natural terrain. One curve should lead to another, creating a feeling of natural harmony.

Most people think that the style of a garden dictates the type of plants to be grown there. While it is true that a traditional formal garden would feature neatly trimmed, compact plants and a rather strict use of color, there certainly are no rules that say it must be so. In fact, a formal garden of straight lines and rectangular beds and borders is one of the best showcases for a diversity of flowers planted in a freewheeling pattern: the formality of the basic design acts as a good counterpoint to the informality of the planting.

After you've decided where to get the best view possible of your garden and whether your plan will be formal or informal, your choice of whether to use beds or borders (or perhaps both) and where to put them will be helped by these considerations.

Beds and borders. The fact that a border is accessible from one side only puts a practical limit to its depth—usually no more than 5 feet. At more than 5 feet deep, it becomes difficult to tend plants in the background without walking on those in the front.

In most home gardens, borders are probably more popular and more practical than beds, and for a simple reason. A bed needs a comparatively large area around it to look its best, and putting one into an average-size garden is a little like placing a large table in the middle of a small room—there's little space left for anything else. You do need space to accommodate beds. Borders, on the other hand, not only conserve space but serve a unique purpose in any garden, by softening the edges of buildings, fences, walkways, and lawns.

Whatever your choice, beds or borders that include a number of different flowering annuals will provide a wealth of color, texture, and interest to any type of garden, formal or informal. With that in mind, and with your basic design in hand, you're ready for the next phase in creating your garden, one that many gardeners find the most enjoyable of all.

Left: A border between a lawn and an evergreen hedge provides the perfect opportunity for a freewheeling display of annual color. Below: A freestanding geometric bed lends itself to a formal planting of silver-gray santolina and maroon coleus.

WHAT TO PLANT

When you get to the stage of choosing what to plant in a bed or border, there are several important preliminary decisions that will influence the look of your garden throughout the year. Because they are essentially decisions based on personal preference, ask yourself these questions before you decide what to plant:

▶Do you want the same color scheme to be constant throughout the growing season, or do you want a changing garden of colors with one wave of blossoms giving way to the next?

▶Do you want a flower garden that is orderly and defined, or an unstructured look more reminiscent of an English cottage garden?

▶Do you want a diversity of plant and flower forms, or plants that are more or less similar in appearance?

▶Does your space limit you to small, compact plants, or can you accommodate some of the rangier, taller-growing annuals to use as background plantings?

▶Do you want a dual-purpose flower garden for both landscape color and cut flowers?

▶Are there any favorite plants that you "must have," or colors that you should not plant because of the color of a background wall, fence, or neighboring plant? There are instances where something as common as a red brick wall or fence will overwhelm various shades of pink flowers. Or perhaps a purple-leafed plum tree with its bronzy foliage will make it unattractive to plant flowers in certain shades of violet or blue.

Depending on how you answer the questions, here are some other factors to think about:

If you want a constant display of the same colors in a bed or border, be sure and choose annuals with a long blooming season: those that bloom early and keep flowering until the first frost in fall. They will minimize the amount of planting and replanting necessary to keep the display going throughout the season. Some of the longest-blooming are sweet alyssum, ageratum, morning glory, impatiens, petunias, marigolds, and zinnias. The Plant Selection Guide will give you more information on the length of bloom for individual flowers.

There are some gardeners who expect more from flower beds and borders than a consistent display of the same combination of colors. These

Above: The perfect pairing of house and garden: the cottage-type architecture of this house is complemented by an old-fashioned border of pink and red dianthus, dwarf yellow marigolds, bushy white and yellow marguerites, and feathery pink astilbe.

A diversity of flower shapes, foliage textures, and color makes for an interesting garden. Pure blue dayflowers, red and pale lavender petunias, the spiky ornamental onion, gloriosa daisies, and an abundance of lush green foliage combine to make a pleasing picture.

usually want an ever-changing garden to entice them out of doors just to see what's coming into bloom next. This garden demands more work, especially in the planning department, but the rewards are definitely there.

The two plans shown are for borders that change colors with the swing of the seasons. As you can see, there is a greater variety of plants in this type of garden than in a static composition. There is also a greater opportunity for combining many different flower and plant forms: plants that are bushy, tall, spindly, or compact; those with spikes of flowers, daisy or cushion-shape blossoms, or those with unusual forms.

If this type of garden appeals to you, think about combining annuals with spikes of flowers, such as stock, snapdragons, salvia, and celosia, with cushion-shape flowers like dwarf asters, marigolds, calendulas, ageratum, geraniums, and phlox. Add to this the various plant forms such as the willowy cosmos, nicotiana, cleome, and love-in-a-mist (*Nigella damascena*), along with the more compact forms of nasturtiums, dianthus, dwarf marigolds, and miniature snapdragons, and you begin to have a bed or border full of diversity and interest.

Plant taller-growing varieties to the rear of lower-growing ones. If annuals of several different heights are to be used, stair-step them from the tallest to the lowest. You might start in the back row with tall cosmos or one of the smaller sunflowers such as the 4-foot 'Picollo', add a few clumps of hollyhocks, then in the middle mass some tall marigolds or zinnias, and end in the front with a combination of ageratum, petunias, lobelia, and alyssum. See the lists for various forms of annuals on pages 32–35.

The Plant Selection Guide in this book (page 57) and the description on the backs of seed packets will also tell you the heights of plants and how far apart to space them. If you like a very abundant, lush look, you can usually get away with spacing them a little closer than recommended; but if you put plants too close together or don't thin them out enough, they will compete with one another for sun, water, root space, and nutrients, and will likely produce inferior flowers.

Using contrasting foliage textures and colors can be as interesting as combining different types of bloom. There are even some annuals whose primary quality is foliage rather than their flowers; for example, amaranthus, dusty miller, the many varieties of coleus, and ornamental cabbage and kale. For more of these unusual annuals, see the list on page 35.

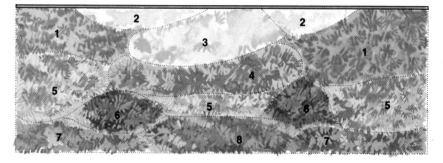

A sample plan for a summer-flowering annual border in shades of blue, orange, and white: 1. blue 'Duchess' asters; 2. 'Italian White' sunflowers; 3. white cosmos; 4. orange cactus-flowered zinnias; 5. 'Orange Lady' marigolds; 'Blue Bedder' salvia; 7. nasturtium 'Gem'; and 8. 'Royal Blazer' ageratum.

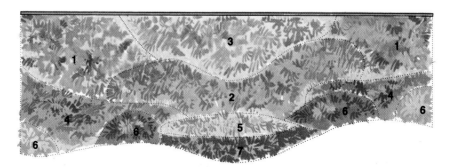

A sample plan for a spring and early-summer border featuring annuals in shades of pink, rose, and white: 1. pink and cherry 'Rocket' snapdragons; 2. pink and rose 'Nicki' nicotiana; 3. pink 'Imperial Giant' stock; 4. rose 'Rhinepearl' primroses; 5. mixed 'Fairy' primroses; 6. 'Raspberry Rose' pansies; and 7. 'Charm' dianthus.

ANNUALS WITH OTHER PLANTS

The border or bed planted entirely with annuals is rare. Because they are not permanent plants, gardeners usually combine annuals with other, more permanent specimens, so there will be something of interest all year.

As many of the photographs in this book testify, some of the favorite combinations are planting annuals and perennials or annuals and spring-flowering bulbs in the same bed. Both perennials and bulbs put in a spectacular show of blossoms—often in colors or forms not found in annuals. By combining the three, then, you not only lengthen the overall period of bloom but also create a scene rich in contrasting flower and foliage forms and expand the possibilities for color combinations.

By adding a few evergreen or deciduous shrubs to the background to the border, you can create a scene with something of interest in every season. Look for shrubs that bloom during periods when little else is flowering in the garden; early-blooming flowering quince and forsythia are good examples. If you live in an area where winter brings a blanket of snow, choose shrubs or trees with appealing winter form or color, such as the birches or dogwoods; or those with fruit that stays on the branches late into the season, such as cotoneasters, crabapples, or firethorns.

There are some gardeners who prefer an even-textured "wall" of greenery behind their beds or borders. For this effect, think about installing a formal hedge instead of a fence, or planting a not-so-formal grouping of leafy evergreen or deciduous shrubs.

In recent years there has been an increase in the popularity of "potpourri" gardens. In the style of the European kitchen gardens, these are working gardens that combine annuals, perennials, herbs, bulbs, vegetables, and even fruit trees. Although they are usually the practical result of trying to grow as many plants as possible in a limited space, the results can be as attractive as they are productive.

ANNUALS AS FILLERS AND SCREENS

There are many situations, especially in the making of new landscapes, where nothing can fill the bill quite like annuals. If you've moved into a new house and just finished the initial landscaping, the garden is liable to look a little bare for the first year or two. In this case, annuals are indispensable. For a nominal investment, you can fill in among immature shrubs and trees with color spots of annuals and create a big improvement in only a little time.

Some ground covers, for example, are notoriously slow to knit into a solid carpet. For the first few years after planting them, many gardeners fill in the bare spots with fast, low-growing annuals such as sweet alyssum, California poppy, or candytuft. Depending on the variety, these may reseed themselves and continue to come up year after year until the ground cover fills in. Another advantage of this method is that any time you should decide to thin them out, or want to eliminate them completely, it's easy to pull or hoe them out before they can set more seed.

If you are renting a house, or know you are not going to be in one location for very long, annuals can provide the look of a glorious garden at far less expense than permanent landscaping. In one short season it's possible to change your outdoor surroundings so much that you would hardly recognize them from before.

One of the most often overlooked plants for quick color are the annual flowering vines. For the most part, they grow at an almost unbelievable rate: the old-fashioned morning glory, scarlet runner bean, and the sweet-scented moonflower (*Calonyction aculeatum*) can, under the right conditions, grow anywhere from 8 to 25 feet in a single season.

As temporary screens against fences, or shade-providers covering arbors or trellises, flowering vines are unequaled. In hot climates, some gardeners even save home cooling costs by using them to screen south and west windows. They can be planted alone or in combination with other, slower-growing but more permanent vines, and in addition to privacy and shade, offer attractive flowers. See page 35 for more suggestions for annual vines.

ANNUALS IN CONTAINERS

Annuals and containers were made for each other. Their fast and easy growth, glamorous display of color, and low cost make them an obvious choice for containers.

There need never be a dull season when you have a few pots of colorful flowers clustered around the door or the patio, or lining a walk. Although it's true that annuals are usually spring- and summer-flowering plants, it's easy to extend color into other

Top: Annuals are good companions to other, more permanent plantings in the garden. Shown here, planted among agapanthus, Shasta daisies, and *Chrysanthemum paludosum* are orange lantanas and gazanias, white petunias, and yellow marigolds. Above: A few pots of dwarf yellow marigolds and silver dusty miller transform this corner into an unexpected delight.

seasons by planting them along with bulbs, perennials, and other flowering plants readily available at the nursery.

Spring pots of primroses and pansies can give way to summer-flowering marigolds and impatiens, and the golden chrysanthemums in fall can be replaced in mild-winter climates with crops of hardy annuals such as linaria and dwarf nasturtium for winter color.

The first thing to do is to purchase a few slightly different-size containers. Garden stores, nurseries, and variety stores are filled with many choices: There are wooden boxes, classic red clay pots, huge half barrels, and an assortment of plastic containers. To minimize the confusion, it's best to limit the number of different types of containers you buy, and to keep the containers relatively the same size.

Experienced container gardeners favor containers in the larger sizes: the bigger they are, the more soil they will hold, which means less frequent watering for the gardener, more root space for the plants, and more chance to experiment with different combinations of flowering plants.

If you purchase clay pots, be sure to hose them down a couple of times to let some water soak in. Clay is very porous and will rob newly planted annuals of their first watering if not allowed to first absorb some water of their own. Cover the drainage holes (but don't completely block them) with broken pieces of pottery, irregularly shaped stones, or, best of all, a small piece of fine mesh screen.

Container basics

You can fill the containers with garden soil, provided it is of good quality with excellent drainage properties; but keep in mind that whatever problems you've had growing plants in your garden soil will only intensify if you use it in containers, especially in the smaller pots. Repeated waterings do tend to compact soil in containers to the point where there may be very little air space left, greatly slowing drainage.

If your soil is marginally acceptable, you can improve it by mixing it in equal proportions with an organic soil amendment such as peat moss, compost, or ground bark soil con-

It's best to use a packaged soil mix for container-grown annuals. 1. Add water directly to the package to ensure thorough wetting. 2. After soaking clay pots in water, place a small piece of fine mesh screen over the drainage hole. 3. Fill the pots with soil, compacting it slightly with your hands, and plant transplants. 4. Water the transplants immediately, using a gentle stream.

ditioner—to make a lighter, looser-growing medium that is more conducive to growing plants in confined quarters. If your soil is downright poor, however, you'll make life easier by using one of the packaged soil mixes sold under a variety of brand names: Jiffy Mix, Redi-Earth, Metro Mix, Super Soil, Pro-Mix, and many others.

Before planting in any container, thoroughly water the soil mass and allow it to settle. After settling, the soil should be I to 3 inches below the rim of the container, depending upon its size. There should be enough space between the rim and soil so that one application of water will moisten the root ball and drain all the way through. If the container is filled with too much soil, watering can become too time-consuming and aggravating a job, requiring several applications for a complete soaking.

Never apply water to container plants in a hard, unbroken stream. In order to protect surface roots and to keep the soil from splashing out, it's best to use a nozzle or water breaker that softens the flow to a gentle, rainlike pattern.

When you pick up plants at the nursery, chances are they will continue to perform as good plants, especially if you transplant them carefully and give them proper care. It is often in the first few days of ownership that plants are mishandled. Keep these points in mind:

▶If you run out of time to plant all of your choices and some plants must be held over till the following weekend, it's easy to let those plants dry out. They probably received a daily watering in the nursery, and should receive the same once they are taken home.

▶Don't plant dry plants. Water before trying to remove them from any type of nursery container. A damp (not wet) root ball won't shatter or stick to the sides of the container.

▶Remove the plants the easy way from cell packs and market packs (2 to I2 plants in a pre-formed plastic flat). Squeeze or push up on the bottom of each cell in the pack to force the root ball above the lip. In removing plants from market trays (those without individual planting spaces), cut the soil in blocks, using a small putty knife or similar tool.

▶Don't pull plants out of containers. Straight-sided metal cans should be cut at the nursery. Plants grown in containers with sloping sides can be eased out by holding the container upside down and tapping the rim on a ledge, being careful with the other hand to protect the root ball from falling out.

CHOOSING ANNUALS FOR CONTAINERS

When it comes time to pick out plants for your containers, there are some important points to keep in mind:

To get the most from your effort, choose annuals with the longest blooming periods.

Choose plants with a compact habit, those that do not need staking. (Of course you can stake tall-growing annuals in a container, but most gardeners find it a nuisance and look for lower-growing varieties of those plants.)

Crowd the plants closer together than you would in the garden. Crowding gives a nice, full effect. (You can compensate for crowding by watering and feeding more often.)

Decide whether you want flowers of all one kind in the container, or several different kinds to create living bouquets. The best bouquet plantings combine several different colors and plant forms. Plant an upright form, a bushy form, and a couple of trailing ones together, and in a few weeks you'll have the diversity of an old-fashioned garden, in miniature. An upright zinnia, a bushy marigold, and trailing lobelia would make a pleasing combination.

Watering and feeding. Because of the limited amount of soil available, plants in containers need more attention than plants in the ground. In hot summer months, daily watering is a common need, especially if the containers receive maximum sun. These repeated waterings have the effect of leaching nutrients out of the soil rather quickly. Most container gardeners favor applying liquid fertilizers at half strength every 2 weeks, rather than full strength monthly, to compensate for this loss.

To keep container specimens looking their best, be sure to pinch off any dead flowers or leaves regularly.

For more detailed information on container gardening of all kinds, be sure to read Ortho's *Container and Hanging Gardens.*

BRINGING ANNUALS INDOORS

In some areas of the country with exceptionally mild winters, many annuals will continue to grow through the seasons. In areas with more severe winters, the first hard frost usually does a complete job of killing them to the ground. Some annuals, though, will respond well to being brought indoors before the first frost. If placed in a location with plenty of light, cut back a little, and fertilized, these can reward the gardener with

Sometimes the only way to add a touch of color in a mature, all-green garden is to hang baskets of shade-loving annuals—such as these fibrous begonias and impatiens—in a thinned-out tree. Bottom: As studied and elegant as any indoor bouquet, this container planting of scarlet nicotiana, pink fibrous begonias and gray *Helichrysum lanatum* is the focal point of this lawnside terrace.

A MOSS-LINED HANGING BASKET

Materials needed: Wire basket (or wire cylinder), sphagnum moss (enough to fill loosely the basket to be lined), a packaged soil mix, four trays of plants (six per tray), and a bowl of water for wetting the moss.

1. Put the moss in a bowl of water to soak. Squeeze the water from a piece of moss 6 inches square and fold it in half—mossy side out. Fit the moss between the top two wires of the basket by squeezing it down. Let it go, and its own springiness will hold it in place. Push the first piece of moss tightly against a vertical wire and insert another piece. Pack in more pieces until this space is tightly filled.

2. Repeat step 1 all the way around the basket. You'll then have a neat, tightly packed collar around the basket between the two top wires. Line the inside of the rest of the basket with generous pieces of moss. Overlap each piece sufficiently so that no soil can leak through. When completely lined, the basket should have an even layer of moss about 1½ inches thick. Trim off straggly moss for a neat, professional appearance.

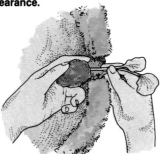

3. Put about 1½ inches of moist soil mix in the bottom of the basket. Poke your fingers through from both sides at soil level and work a hole large enough to insert a plant, spreading the wires a bit if necessary.

4. Insert each plant so that its rootball lies on the soil mix surface and the crown of the plant is even with the inside of the moss lining.

5. When the first row of plants is in place, cover it with an inch or two of soil mix and add another row of plants. Keep adding soil and plants until you reach the collar of the moss at the top.

6. Finally, fill all but about an inch of the basket with soil mix and plant the top as you would a flower pot. Use several plants with about the same spacing as on the sides.

winter blooms, until short days and the dry heat of the house make them decline.

When the weather warms in the following spring, the overwintered plants can be returned to the outdoors, to grow on in containers or even be transplanted into the ground.

See page 33 for a list of annuals that can be brought indoors in winter.

ANNUALS IN HANGING BASKETS

There was a time when hanging baskets generally appealed to two types of gardeners: one was simply fascinated with hanging and trailing plants; the other had so little ground space that hanging baskets were one of the few ways to have some flowering color. While hanging baskets are the best way to display plants with a trailing habit, they are no longer limited to those varieties alone. The moss-lined wire basket has made it possible to grow almost any annual, no matter what its habit, as a hanging display. See the list on page 33 for some specific suggestions.

Growing annuals in hanging baskets is a special form of container gardening. The basics of soil, water, and fertilizers are the same, but depending largely on what type of basket you choose, there are some special considerations. The choice of hanging containers varies from clay and plastic pots to wooden containers of all shapes, wicker and bamboo baskets, and the moss-lined wire baskets.

Once you hang any container made of a porous material (clay, wood, wicker, or moss), additional surface is exposed to air circulation and the wind, sun, and dry air evaporate water from the soil faster than from a container on the ground. In very warm, dry, or windy areas of the country, flowers can sunburn or dry out in a matter of hours. Gardeners compensate somewhat by hanging the baskets in areas protected from wind and afternoon sun. Plastic containers do a better job of retaining soil moisture; but many people find them aesthetically lacking and thus not altogether appropriate for garden display.

Because hanging baskets dry out so quickly, the main consideration as you plan a hanging garden is how to water them on a regular basis. One of the best ways is to take the container down and set it up to its rim in a bucket of water until it is thoroughly soaked through. If you use this method, make sure your containers, with soil, are light in weight; otherwise, hanging them securely may be a problem, and lifting them up and down for watering can be a back-breaking difficult task.

Moss-lined baskets. What makes the moss-lined wire basket stand out from other hanging containers is that it can be planted in the sides as well as the top. This makes it possible to plant almost any annual you desire for large, profuse displays of hanging color. See the accompanying illustrations for the steps involved in making a moss-lined hanging basket.

To keep the basket neat in and full color requires continuous grooming. Remove all spent flowers, prune off any shoots that stray, and fertilize and water regularly, the same as will other container plants. You'll find that a few old-fashioned hairpins will come in handy for pinning errant shoots and vines to the moss.

THE CUTTING GARDEN

An extra, but often overlooked, dimension of flower gardening is the cutting garden. With it you can bring the colors and fragrances of gardens indoors, not just for special occasions, but for everyday enjoyment.

The idea of establishing a separate garden for the sole purpose of providing cut flowers is an old-fashioned one, but one that deserves a second look. Years ago, when the average garden was much larger and time not quite so hurried, the cutting garden was the obvious answer for supplying armloads of flowers without disturbing the rest of the garden. Even today, many homeowners find themselves with a seldom-used side yard that lends itself beautifully to the purpose.

Traditionally, cutting gardens are set apart from the rest of the garden and laid out in convenient rows, similar to the vegetable garden. The site should receive at least a half day of direct sun and the soil should be prepared as for any other garden (see page 47). If the soil is too poor, or if you simply favor the convenience, consider installing raised beds, which, among their other advantages, simplify watering and weeding.

Annuals are perfect candidates for the cutting garden: in almost every instance, the more you cut them, the more they bloom. The easiest approach to selecting annuals for cut flowers is to buy and plant a packet of seeds of mixed kinds especially selected for cutting. Such readymade mixes will give you a range of spike forms, round, and filler flowers; pastels, whites, and bright colors—even some with fragrance. All will stay fresh for 4 to 10 days if properly cut and maintained.

Cutting the flowers. The longevity of cut flowers can be increased by following a few simple rules.

Generally speaking, flowers should be cut in the morning or evening when they are plump with water; flowers cut in the middle of the day are often somewhat wilted and, once cut, have difficulty absorbing enough water.

Always use a *sharp* knife or pair of scissors to make the cleanest cut possible.

Take a bucket or pail of water into the garden and plunge the stems into the water immediately after cutting.

When you are ready to arrange the flowers, remove any foliage from the bases of stems to prevent the water in the vase from fouling too quickly. Professional flower arrangers often cut the stems a second time before putting them into the vase. For the longest life, they advise cutting the flowers underwater, and making the cut at an angle.

Place the arrangement in a cool room, away from direct sunlight, and change the water daily.

In addition to brightening your home, fresh flowers from your own garden make special gifts for friends and neighbors. And because the cutting garden is essentially a utilitarian one, it's a perfect spot to try new and unusual annuals that you might hesitate to try in more visible or more formal areas.

If your cutting garden produces an abundance of flowers, you might also consider selling the surplus: some specialty florists often want unusual flowers from home gardens.

Top: The rewards of a cutting garden— a basket full of long-stemmed statice, snapdragons, and gerbera daisies. Above: If you have the room, an old-fashioned cutting garden can provide armloads of flowers for indoor arrangements. This garden specializes in long-stemmed varieties of marigolds and snapdragons and a large bed of white, lacy baby's breath.

COMMON FLOWER SHAPES

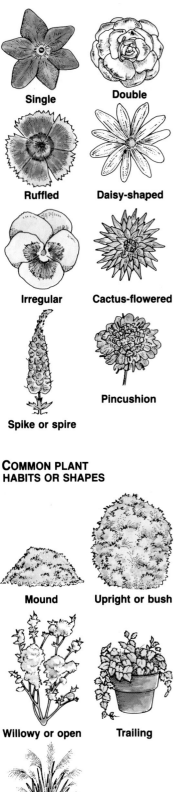

Single **Double**

Ruffled **Daisy-shaped**

Irregular **Cactus-flowered**

Pincushion

Spike or spire

COMMON PLANT HABITS OR SHAPES

Mound **Upright or bush**

Willowy or open **Trailing**

Vertical accent

AN ANNUAL INVENTORY: SELECTED LISTS

For that special purpose, problem, or form, the following categories are designed to help make your planning easier and more fun. For those plants that interest you, refer to the Plant Selection Guide for additional information. Remember that just because a plant appears on a list doesn't mean that all varieties necessarily fit that category. In many cases only selected varieties match the description. The final list of this section is a small selection of some mail-order firms from which you can order seed and catalogs.

HARDY ANNUAL

These frost-tolerant flowers can be sown outdoors in very early spring.

Arctotis stoechadifolia var. *grandis* (African Daisy)
Brassica coerula (Ornamental Cabbage and Kale; best sown in summer for fall display)
Calendula officinalis (Pot Marigold)
Centauria cyanus (Bachelor Button)
Cheiranthus cheiri (Wallflower)
Clarkia hybrids (Godetia; Farewell-to-Spring; tolerates light frosts)
Consolida ambigua (Larkspur)
Cynoglossum amabile (Chinese Forget-Me-Not)
Eschscholzia californica (California Poppy)
Grasses:
   Agrostis nebulosa (Cloud Grass)
   Avena sterilis (Animated Oats)
   Briza maxima (Quaking Grass)
   Lagurus ovatus (Hare's Tail Grass)
Gypsophila elegans (Baby's Breath)
Lathyrus odorata (Sweet Pea)
Lavatera hybrids (Tree Mallow)
Linaria maroccana (Toadflax)
Lobularia maritima (Sweet Alyssum)
Nemophila menziesii (Baby Blue Eyes)
Nigella damascena (Love-in-a-Mist)
Papaver rhoeas (Field Poppy)
Papaver nudicaule (Iceland Poppy)
Phlox drummondii (Annual Phlox)
Reseda odorata (Mignonette)
Viola × *wittrockiana* (Pansy)

HALF-HARDY ANNUALS (OUTDOOR SOWING)

Annuals that are easy to sow directly into the ground outdoors, but should not be sown until all danger of frost has passed.

Cataranthus roseus (Madagascar Periwinkle)
Convolvulus tricolor (Dwarf Morning Glory)
Coreopsis tinctoria (Calliopsis)
Cosmos bipinnatus (Mexican Aster)
Cosmos sulphureous (Orange Cosmos)
Dianthus chinensis (China Pink)
Dianthus barbatus (Sweet William)
Euphorbia marginata (Snow-on-the-Mountain)
Helianthus species (Sunflower)
Iberis species (Candytuft)
Ipomea species (Morning Glory; Cardinal Vine; Cypress Vine)
Mirabilis jalapa (Four o'Clock)
Nicotiana alba (Flowering Tobacco)
Portulaca grandiflora (Rose Moss)
Ricinus communis (Castor Bean)
Sanvitalia procumbens (Creeping Zinnia)
Scabiosa atropurpurea (Pincushion Flower)
Tagetes patula (French Marigold)
Trachymene coerulea (Blue Lace Flower)
Tropaeolum majus (Nasturtium)
Zea mays var. *japonica* (Ornamental Corn)
Zinnia species (Zinnia)

HALF-HARDY ANNUALS (INDOOR SOWING)

Annuals that are best when started ahead indoors.

Ageratum houstonianum (Floss Flower)
Alcea rosea (Hollyhock)
Amaranthus tricolor (Jacob's Coat)
Amaranthus caudatus (Love-Lies Bleeding)
Anchusa capensis (Cape Forget-Me-Not)
Antirrhinum majus (Snapdragon)
Arctotis stoechidifolia var. *grandis* (African Daisy)
Begonia × *semperflorens-cultorum* (Wax-leaf Begonia)
Brachycome iberidifolia (Swan River Daisy)
Browallia speciosa (Sapphire Flower)
Callistephus chinensis (China Aster)
Campanula medium (Canterbury Bells)
Capsicum annuum (Ornamental Pepper)
Cataranthus roseus (Madagascar Periwinkle)
Celosia cristata (Cockscomb)
Cleome hasslerana (Spider Flower)
Coleus × *hybridus* (Coleus)
Consolida ambigua (Larkspur)
Coreopsis tinctoria (Calliopsis)
Cosmos bipinnatus (Mexican Aster)
Cosmos sulphureous (Orange Cosmos)
Cuphea ignea (Firecracker Plant)
Dahlia hybrids (Dahlia)
Dianthus barbatus (Sweet William)
Dianthus chinensis (China Pink)
Dimorphotheca sinuata (Cape Marigold)
Dyssodia tenuiloba (Dahlberg Daisy)
Euphorbia marginata (Snow-on-the-Mountain)
Gaillardia pulchella (Blanket Flower)
Gazania rigens (Gazania)
Gerbera jamesonii (Transvaal Daisy)
Gomphrena globosa (Globe Amaranth)
Grasses:
   Coix lacryma-jobi (Job's Tears)
   Pennisetum setaceum (Crimson Fountain Grass)
   Rhynchlytrum roseum (Ruby Grass)
   Setaria macrostachya (Plains Bristle Grass)
Helichrysum bracteatum (Strawflower)
Heliotropium arborescens (Heliotrope)
Impatiens balsamina (Balsam)
Impatiens wallerana (Busy Lizzie; Impatiens)
Kochia scoparia (Summer Cypress; Burning Bush)
Limonium bonduellii (Algerian Sea Lavender)
Limonium sinuatum (Notch-leaf Sea Lavender)
Lobelia erinus (Edging Lobelia)
Matthiola incana (Stock)
Mimulus × *hybridus* (Monkey Flower)
Mirabilis jalapa (Four o'Clock)
Nemesia strumosa (Pouch Nemesia)

Nicotiana alba (Flowering Tobacco)
Nierembergia hippomanica (Cup Flower)
Pelargonium × hortorum (Geranium)
Petunia × hybrida (Petunia)
Rudbeckia hirta var. *pulcherrima* (Gloriosa Daisy)
Salpiglossis sinuata (Painted Tongue)
Salvia farinacea (Blue Sage)
Salvia splendens (Scarlet Sage)
Schizanthus × wisetonensis (Poor Man's Orchid)
Senecio cineraria (Dusty Miller)
Tagetes erecta (African Marigold)
Tagetes, triploid strains (Triploid Marigolds)
Thunbergia alata (Black-eyed Susan Vine)
Tithonia rotundifolia (Mexican Sunflower)
Torenia fournieri (Wishbone Flower)
Verbena × hybrida (Garden Verbena)
Viola × wittrockiana (Pansy)

TENDER ANNUALS
Annuals that should not be set out or sown outdoors until the soil is thoroughly warm.

Amaranthus tricolor (Jacob's Coat)
Amaranthus caudatus (Love-Lies-Bleeding)
Celosia cristata (Cockscomb)
Heliotropium arborescens (Heliotrope)

ANNUALS THAT NATURALIZE
Alcea rosea (Hollyhock)
Anchusa capensis (Cape Forget-Me-Not)
Antirrhinum majus (Snapdragon)
Calendula officinalis (Pot Marigold)
Campanula medium (Canterbury Bells)
Coreopsis tinctoria (Calliopsis)
Cosmos bipinnatus (Mexican Aster)
Cosmos sulphureous (Orange Cosmos)
Cynoglossum amabile (Chinese Forget-Me-Not)
Dianthus chinensis (China Pink)
Dyssodia tenuiloba (Dahlberg Daisy)
Eschscholzia californica (California Poppy)
Euphorbia marginata (Snow-on-the-Mountain)
Grasses:
   Agrostis nebulosa (Cloud Grass)
   Coix lacryma-jobi (Job's Tears)
   Eragrostis abyssinica (Love Grass)
   Pennisetum setaceum (Crimson Fountain Grass, reseeds in zones 8–10)
   Setaria macrostachya (Plains Bristle Grass)
Kochia scoparia forma *trichophylla* 'Childsii' (Summer Cypress; Burning Bush)
Linaria maroccana (Toadflax)
Lobularia maritima (Sweet Alyssum)
Mirabilis jalapa (Four o'Clock)
Molucella laevis (Bells of Ireland)
Myosotis sylvatica (Forget-Me-Not)
Nigella damascena (Love-in-a-Mist)
Papaver rhoeas (Field Poppy)
Papaver nudicaule (Iceland Poppy)
Portulaca grandiflora (Rose Moss)

COOL-SUMMER ANNUALS
Brachycome iberidifolia (Swan River Daisy)
Cheiranthus cheiri (Wallflower)
Clarkia hybrids (Godetia; Farewell-to-Spring)
Consolida ambigua (Rocket Larkspur)
Lathyrus odorata (Sweet Pea)
Linaria maroccana (Toadflax)
Matthiola incana (Stock)
Mimulus × hybridus (Monkey Flower)
Nemesia strumosa (Pouch Nemesia)

Papaver nudicaule (Iceland Poppy)
Salpiglossis sinuata .(Painted Tongue)
Schizanthus × wisetonensis (Poor Man's Orchid)
Tropaeolum majus (Nasturtium)
Viola × wittrockiana (Pansy)

HEAT-TOLERANT ANNUALS
Amaranthus species (Jacob's Coat; Love-Lies-Bleeding)
Begonia × semperflorens-cultorum (Wax-leaf Begonia)
Capsicum annuum (Ornamental Pepper)
Cataranthus roseus (Madagascar Periwinkle)
Celosia cristata (Cockscomb)
Convolvulus tricolor (Dwarf Morning Glory)
Coreopsis tinctoria (Calliopsis)
Cuphea ignea (Mexican Cigar Plant)
Dahlia hybrids (Dahlia)
Dyssodia tenuiloba (Dahlberg Daisy)
Euphorbia marginata (Snow-on-the-Mountain)
Gomphrena globosa (Globe Amaranth)
Grasses, all grasses
Helianthus species (Sunflowers)
Kochia scoparia forma *trichophylla* 'Childsii' (Summer Cypress; Burning Bush)
Mirabilis jalapa (Four o'Clock)
Petunia × hybrida (Petunia)
Portulaca grandiflora (Rose Moss)
Ricinus communis (Castor Bean)
Rudbeckia hirta (Gloriosa Daisy)
Salvia species (Sage)
Sanvitalia procumbens (Creeping Zinnia)
Senecio cineraria (Dusty Miller)
Tagetes Triploid strains (Triploid Marigolds)
Tithonia rotundifolia (Mexican Sunflower)
Verbena × hybrida (Garden Verbena)
Zinnia species (Zinnia)

DROUGHT-TOLERANT ANNUALS
Amaranthus tricolor (Jacob's Coat)
Arctotis stoechadifolia var. *grandis* (African Daisy)
Cataranthus roseus (Madagascar Periwinkle)
Convolvulus tricolor (Dwarf Morning Glory)
Coreopsis tinctoria (Calliopsis)
Dimorphotheca sinuata (Cape Marigold)
Dyssodia teniuloba (Dahlberg Daisy)
Eschscholzia californica (California Poppy)
Euphorbia marginata (Snow-on-the-Mountain)
Gazania rigens (Gazania)
Gomphrena globosa (Globe Amaranth)
Kochia scoparia forma *trichophylla* 'Childsii' (Summer Cypress; Burning Bush)
Limonium species (Sea Lavender)
Lobularia maritima (Sweet Alyssum)
Mirabilis jalapa (Four o'Clock)
Portulaca grandiflora (Rose Moss)
Salvia species (Sage)
Sanvitalia procumbens (Creeping Zinnia)
Senecio cineraria (Dusty Miller)
Tithonia rotundifolia (Mexican Sunflower)

ANNUALS FOR MOIST SOIL
Since most annuals only *tolerate* very moist soil, * indicates the plant will thrive in it.

Cataranthus roseus (Madagascar Periwinkle)
Cleome hasslerana (Spider Flower)
Euphorbia marginata (Snow-on-the-Mountain)

*Mimulus × hybridus (Monkey Flower)
*Myosotis sylvatica (Forget-Me-Not)
Ricinus communis (Castor Bean)
Torenia fournieri (Wishbone Flower)
Tropaeolum majus (Nasturtium)
Viola × wittrockiana (Pansy)

ANNUALS FOR SHADE
These annuals will tolerate partial shade. (* indicates those that are most tolerant of shade)

Begonia × semperflorens-cultorum (Wax-leaf Begonia)
Browallia speciosa (Sapphire Flower)
Campanula medium (Canterbury Bells)
*Coleus × hybridus (Coleus)
*Impatiens wallerana (Busy Lizzie; Impatiens)
*Mimulus × hybridus (Monkey Flower)
Myosotis sylvatica (Forget-Me-Not)
Nemophila menziesii (Baby Blue Eyes)
Nicotiana alba (Flowering Tobacco)
Salvia splendens (Scarlet Sage)
Thunbergia alata (Black-eyed Susan Vine)
*Torenia fournieri (Wishbone Flower)
Viola × wittrockiana (Pansy)

ANNUALS FOR INDOORS
Annuals that can be brought inside in winter.

Amaranthus tricolor (Jacob's Coat)
Amaranthus caudatus (Love-Lies-Bleeding)
Begonia × semperflorens-cultorum (Wax-leaf Begonia)
Browallia speciosa (Sapphire Flower)
Capsicum annuum (Ornamental Pepper)
Cataranthus roseus (Madagascar Periwinkle)
Coleus × hybridus (Coleus)
Cuphea ignea (Mexican Cigar Plant)
Gazania rigens (Gazania)
Heliotropium arborescens (Heliotrope)
Impatiens wallerana (Busy Lizzie; Impatiens)
Pelargonium × hortorum (Geranium)
Thunbergia alata (Black-eyed Susan Vine)
Torenia fournieri (Wishbone Flower)

ANNUALS FOR FRAGRANCE
Brachycome iberidifolia (Swan River Daisy)
Cheiranthus cheiri (Wallflower)
Dianthus barbatus (Sweet William)
Heliotropium arborescens (Heliotrope)
Lathyrus odoratus (Sweet Pea)
Lobularia maritima (Sweet Alyssum)
Matthiola incana (Stock)
Mirabilis jalapa (Four o'Clock)
Reseda odorata (Mignonette)

ANNUALS FOR HANGING BASKETS
Browallia speciosa (Sapphire Flower)
Impatiens wallerana (Busy Lizzie; Impatiens)
Lobelia erinus (Edging Lobelia)
Pelargonium × hortorum (Geranium)
Petunia × hybrida, cascade forms (Petunia)
Sanvitallia procumbens (Creeping Zinnia)
Thunbergia alata (Black-eyed Susan Vine)
Tropaeolum majus (Nasturtium)
Verbena × hybrida (Garden Verbena)

ANNUALS FOR EDGING
These flowers have forms and flowers ideal for edging beds and borders.

Ageratum houstonianum (Floss Flower)
Antirrhinum majus (Snapdragon)

Begonia × *semperflorens-cultorum* (Waxleaf Begonia)
Brassica olereacea (Ornamental Cabbage, Kale)
Browallia speciosa (Sapphire Flower)
Callistephus chinensis (China Aster)
Capsicum annuum (Ornamental Pepper)
Convolvulus tricolor (Dwarf Morning Glory)
Cuphea ignea (Mexican Cigar Plant)
Dianthus chinensis (China Pink)
Iberis species (Candytuft)
Impatiens wallerana (Busy Lizzie; Impatiens)
Linaria maroccana (Toadflax)
Lobelia erinus (Edging Lobelia)
Nierembergia hippomanica (Cup Flower)
Phlox drummondii (Annual Phlox)
Petunia × *hybrida* (Petunia)
Senecio cineraria (Dusty Miller)
Tagetes 'Irish Lace' (Irish Lace Marigold)
Tagetes patula (French Marigold)
Torenia fournieri (Wishbone Flower)
Viola × *wittrockiana* (Pansy)
Zinnia, dwarf forms (Zinnia)

VERTICAL ANNUALS

These annuals are best for spikey, vertical effects in the garden.

Alcea rosea (Hollyhock)
Antirrhinum majus (Snapdragon)
Campanula medium (Canterbury Bells)
Celosia cristata, plume types (Cockscomb)
Consolida ambigua (Larkspur)
Grasses:
   Coix lacryma-jobi (Job's Tears)
   Lagurus ovatus (Hare's Tail Grass)
   Pennisetum setaceum (Crimson Fountain Grass)

Low-growing, vertical, and bushy plant shapes are skillfully combined in an informal patio border.

Setaria macrostachya (Plains Bristle Grass)
Zea mays var. *japonica* (Ornamental Corn)
Matthiola incana (Stock)
Molucella laevis (Bells of Ireland)
Nicotiana alba (Flowering Tobacco)
Reseda odorata (Mignonette)
Salvia species (Sage)

LOW-GROWING ANNUALS

These annuals have a low form useful in the foregound of the bed or border, or as ground covers. (* indicates spreading forms useful for ground covers)

Ageratum houstanianum (Floss Flower)
Antirrhinum majus (Snapdragon)
*Arctotis (African Daisy)
Begonia × *semperflores-cultorum* (Waxleaf Begonia)
Calendula officinalis (Pot Marigold)
Capsicum annuum (Ornamental Pepper)
Cataranthus roseus (Madagascar Periwinkle)
Celosia cristata (Cockscomb)
Coleus × *hybridus* (Coleus)
Cuphea ignea (Mexican Cigar Plant)
Dahlia hybrids (Dahlia)
*Dimorphotheca sinuata (Cape Marigold)
*Dyssodia tenuiloba (Dahlberg Daisy)
Gaillardia pulchella (Blanket Flower)
*Gazania rigens (Gazania)
Gerbera jamesonii (Transvaal Daisy)
Iberis species (Candytuft)
Impatiens wallerana (Busy Lizzie; Impatiens)
Linaria maroccana (Toadflax)
Lobelia erinus (Edging Lobelia)
*Lobularia maritima (Sweet Alyssum)
Myosotis sylvatica (Forget-Me-Not)
Nemesia strumosa (Pouch Nemesia)
Nemophila menziesii (Baby Blue Eyes)
Nicotiana alba (Flowering Tobacco)

Nierembergia hippomanica (Cup Flower)
Papaver species (Poppy)
Pelargonium × *hortorum* (Geranium)
Phlox drummondii (Annual Phlox)
Petunia × *hybrida* (Petunia)
*Portulaca grandiflora (Rose Moss)
Salvia species (Sage)
*Sanvitalia procumbens (Creeping Zinnia)
Schizanthus × *wisetonensis* (Poor Man's Orchid)
Senecio cineraria (Dusty Miller)
Tagetes species (Marigolds)
Tropaeolum majus (Nasturtium)
Verbena × *hybrida* (Garden Verbena)
Viola × *wittrockiana* (Pansy)
Zinnia species (Zinnia)

ROUNDED ANNUALS

These plants are rounded to vase-shape, dense, and of medium size, for the middle of the border. (* indicates annuals especially useful for temporary hedges)

Anchusa capensis (Cape Forget-Me-Not)
*Amaranthus tricolor (Jacob's Coat)
Calendula officinalis (Pot Marigold)
Callistephus chinensis (China Aster)
Cataranthus rosea (Madagascar Periwinkle)
Cheiranthus cheiri (Wallflower)
Clarkia hybrids (Godetia; Farewell-to-Spring)
*Cleome hasslerana (Spider Flower)
Coleus × *hybridus* (Coleus)
Convolvulus tricolor (Dwarf Morning Glory)
Coreopsis tinctoria (Calliopsis)
Dahlia hybrids (Dahlia)
Dianthus barbatus (Sweet William)
Eschscholzia californica (California Poppy)
*Euphorbia marginata (Snow-on-the-Mountain)
Gomphrena globosa (Globe Amaranth)

Grasses:
  Avena sterilis (Animated Oats)
  Agrostis nebulosa (Cloud Grass)
  Briza maxima (Quaking Grass)
  Eragrostis abyssinica (Love Grass)
  Pennisetum setaceum (Crimson Fountain Grass)
  Rhynchelytrum roseum (Ruby Grass)
  Setaria macrostachya (Plains Bristle Grass)
Gypsophila elegans (Annual Baby's Breath)
Helianthus species, dwarf varieties (Sunflowers)
Helichrysum bracteatum (Strawflower)
Heliotropium arborescens (Heliotrope)
Impatiens wallerana (Busy Lizzie, Impatiens)
*Ipomea leptophylla (Bush Morning Glory)
Kochia scoparia forma *trichophylla* 'Childsii' (Summer Cypress)
Lavatera hybrids (Tree Mallow)
Limonium species (Sea Lavender)
Mirabilis jalapa (Four o'Clock)
Pelargonium × *hortorum* (Geranium)
Petunia × *hybrida* (Petunia)
Rudbeckia hirta (Gloriosa Daisy)
Schizanthus × *wisetonensis* (Poor Man's Orchid).
Tagetes species (Marigolds)
Zinnia elegans (Zinnia)

TALL-GROWING ANNUALS

These annuals are useful for backgrounds.

Alcea rosea (Hollyhock)
Amaranthus tricolor (Jacob's Coat)
Cleome hasslerana (Spider Flower)
Helianthus species (Sunflower)
Ricinus communis (Castor Bean)
Tithonia rotundifolia (Mexican Sunflower)
Zea mays var. *japonica* (Ornamental Corn)
Zinnia elegans, tallest varieties (Zinnia)

OPEN ANNUALS

These annuals have open, loose forms and are of medium height. They are best mixed into the border.

Brachycome iberidifolia (Swan River Daisy)
Centauria cyanus (Bachelor Button)
Coreopsis tinctoria (Calliopsis)
Cosmos bipinnatus (Mexican Aster)
Cosmos sulphureous (Orange Cosmos)
Cynoglossum amabile (Chinese Forget-Me-Not)
Lagurus ovatus (Hare's Tail Grass)
Helichrysum bracteatum (Strawflower)
Nigella damascena (Love-in-a-Mist)
Papaver species (Poppy)
Reseda odorata (Mignonette)
Salpiglossis sinuata (Painted Tongue)
Scabiosa atropurpurea (Pincushion Flower)
Trachymene coerulea (Blue Lace Flower)

FOLIAGE ANNUALS

These annuals have particularly attractive foliage.

Amaranthus tricolor (Jacob's Coat)
Amaranthus caudatus (Love-Lies-Bleeding)
Begonia × *semperflorens-cultorum* (Wax-leaf Begonia)
Brassica oleracea acephela (Ornamental Kale)
Brassica oleracea capitata (Ornamental Cabbage)
Coleus × *hybridus* (Coleus)

Euphorbia marginata (Snow-on-the-Mountain)
Ipomea species (Morning Glory)
Kochia scoparia forma *trichophylla* 'Childsii' (Summer Cypress; Burning Bush)
Pelargonium × *hortorum* (Geranium)
Ricinus communis (Castor Bean)
Senecio cineraria (Dusty Miller)
Tagetes 'Irish Lace' (Irish Lace Marigold)
Thunbergia alata (Black-eyed Susan Vine)
Zea mays var. *japonica* (Ornamental Corn)

ANNUAL VINES

Ipomea alba (Moonflower Vine)
Ipomea × *multifida* (Cardinal Climber)
Ipomea quamoclit (Cypress Vine)
Ipomea nil; I. purpurea; I. tricolor (Morning Glory)
Lathyrus odorata (Sweet Pea)
Thunbergia alata (Black-eyed Susan Vine)
Tropaeolum majus (Nasturtium; if trained)

A SELECTED LIST OF MAJOR SUPPLIERS FOR SEEDS AND CATALOGS

Burpee Seed Co.
300 Park Avenue
Warminster, PA 18974

Farmer Seed & Nursery Co.
818 NW 4th Street
Faribault, Minn. 55021

Henry Field Seed & Nursery Co.
Shenandoah, Iowa 51602

Gurney Seed Co.
Yankton, South Dakota 57079

Joseph Harris Co., Inc.
Moreton Farm
Rochester, NY 14624

Herbst Brothers Seedsmen, Inc.
1000 N. Main St.
Brewster, NY 10509

J.W. Jung Seed Co.
Randolph, Wisc. 53956

Meyer Seed Co.
600 S. Caroline Street
Baltimore, MD 21231

Nichols Garden Nursery
1190 N. Pacific Highway
Albany, Oregon 97321

L.L. Olds Seed Co.
P.O. Box 7790
2901 Packers Ave.
Madison, Wisc. 53707

Geo. W. Park Seed Co., Inc.
P.O. Box 31
Greenwood, S.C. 29647

Reuter Seed Co.
320 N. Carrollton Ave.
New Orleans, LA 70119

R.H. Shumway Seedsman, Inc.
628 Cedar St.
Rockford, Ill. 61101

Stokes Seeds, Inc.
737 Main St.
Box 548
Buffalo, NY 14240

Thompson & Morgan, Inc.
P.O. Box 100
Farmingdale, NJ 07727

Otis Twilley Seed Co., Inc.
P.O. Box 65
Trevose, PA 19047

W.J. Unwin Ltd
P.O. Box 9
Farmingdale, NJ 07727

In a few short weeks, these annual morning glory vines can cover a wall to create privacy, coolness, and beauty. Middle: Annuals grown for their foliage effects can be as outstanding as any flower variety. Shown here, a simple but effective combination of dusty miller, castor bean, and crimson fountain grass. Bottom: A mixed planting of annuals fills in among this shady green border.

STARTING ANNUALS FROM SEED

The amount of time and equipment needed to start annuals from seed is minimal compared to the rewards. Ask any gardener who has tried it, and you're likely to hear nothing but enthusiastic replies.

Ask yourself what kind of gardener you think you are. If you're the type who really enjoys gardening, and gets satisfaction out of the whole process from beginning to end, you'll want to start at least part of your garden from seed.

Starting any plant from seed is an immensely satisfying experience. With annuals it's even more enjoyable because they are generally easy to start, not overly particular about growing conditions, and, best of all, can produce spectacular results in just a short time.

A walk through your garden on an afternoon in the height of summer can be even more rewarding when you recall that a few weeks earlier, the colorful display was only a handful of pots and trays lined up in a sunny window. The 7-foot hollyhocks, masses of nasturtiums, marigolds, and vibrant zinnias all shared an inconspicuous beginning with a few seed packets, some potting soil, and the desire to make your surroundings more beautiful.

Apart from the sense of accomplishments, there are some practical reasons for starting annuals from seed.

When you buy transplants at a nursery or garden center, you can be reasonably sure of high quality and good performance in the garden; but the fact remains that you will be locked into whatever choices of plants you see before you. In order to make the job easier and more profita-

At times the only way you can get the special varieties of flowers you want is to start them from seed. The seeds of these Transvaal daisies were ordered from a specialty catalog.

ble for the commercial grower, the nursery owner, and the home gardener, the plants most commonly grown are the "sure-bets"—those that are most popular, that hold up well in cell packs or flats, and those hardy varieties guaranteed to survive a "brown thumb." This is to the good, but *you* may want *your* garden to be more. By complementing nursery supplies with seeds offered by good catalogs, you can have a much wider assortment, including more unusual, even rare, varieties. Your garden will become even more personal and distinctive.

Another most important advantage of seed is that you can time planting precisely to correspond with your own individual climate. Many gardeners find the sight of tender annuals in the nursery early in the season irresistible and go ahead and plant them outdoors when it's really not yet warm enough. Once planted too early, they rarely regain their full vigor, and second plantings are often necessary for a good display of flowers.

In many northern states, bedding plants are difficult to find after mid-June, especially in choices gardeners want for late bloom. Many gardeners there meet the problem by learning how to grow from seed. In these states, starting from seed is also much easier to do at this time of year than in early spring, when light levels are low and windows cold.

Last but not least, starting annuals from seed is the least expensive way to produce a flower garden. Ten dollars' worth of seeds can provide any gardener with a wide selection of plants, probably more than it will be possible to plant.

Commercial seed fields filled with zinnias show well the color and brilliance that annuals have to offer.

The germination process is a miracle no gardener ever tires of witnessing. By satisfying a few basic requirements, anybody can have success starting annuals from seed.

BEFORE YOU GET STARTED

Before you put that first seed into the soil, a little general information will help you off in the right direction.

What is a seed? This may seem a ridiculous question, but the answer will give you important clues on how to best treat seeds.

A seed is a fertilized "egg," somewhat like the fertilized egg a chicken produces. Inside the outer protective coating of a seed is the embryo—a highly miniaturized and simplified version of the adult plant. Between the protective outer coating and the embryo itself is food stored in quantities sufficient to nourish the plant until it has enough roots and leaves to absorb nutrients from the soil. The amount stored obviously varies by size.

After the seed is produced, it needs a period of rest or dormancy in order to germinate. During this period the food in the seed changes to a form useful to the embryo. Seeds of different plants need varying lengths of dormancy, but for most annual seeds, the period from the end of the growing season (fall) to the next spring is sufficient.

In order to germinate, a seed needs moisture, air, and favorable temperatures. The germination process is the same, no matter what method you use to start it. Once the seed absorbs water, the food surrounding the embryo converts from starch to a sugar, and the embryo starts to grow. Soon the miniature plant is too large for the confines of the seed, and breaks through the softened outer shell and begins to take its nourishment from the outside environment.

As you can imagine, this is a critical time in the life of a plant, and there are many steps a gardener can take to make this process a success. Several time-tested methods of starting seeds are outlined in this section.

Anything you can do to make seeds germinate rapidly and grow quickly will increase their chances of growing into vigorous plants.

Seed catalogs. The catalogs seed companies put out each year can be a great source of inspiration, ideas, and information for gardeners of every level of experience. Catalogs featuring spring- and summer- flowering annuals are mailed in the fall and winter months to those who request them, usually in plenty of time to place and receive orders before the planting season. On a drab winter day, the arrival of a seed catalog, filled with colorful pictures and remarkable descriptions, can be just what the gardener needs: hope and enticement toward an even more beautiful garden in the months ahead.

See the list on page 35 for catalogs you can send for. It is by no means a complete list, so be sure and take a look at home and garden magazine advertisements for other sources. Many catalogs will be sent free of charge, others for a nominal fee that is usually refunded with the first order. And remember, there's no sense skimping on second-quality seed: the best seeds from a reliable source will always return your investment many times over.

As a general rule, also be wary of mail offers of "amazing plants" that sound too good to be true. They probably are.

General tips. After you buy and plant seeds, it may seem wise to save the leftovers from one year to the next; but in fact, it's better to go ahead and plant them all, or give the excess to a gardening friend. While it's true that some seeds remain viable for many years, the cost of fresh, guaranteed seed is so low that it really isn't worth risking the time and effort for a poor stand of weak seedlings.

The general rule of thumb is to plant twice as many seeds as you think you need. Some seeds just won't germinate. Some seedlings will be weak and need to be thinned out, or simply won't make it through the transplanting procedure.

Another rule of thumb is to gauge the depth of planting by the size of the seed itself. There is a great range in the size of seeds, from the minute begonia and petunia, to the large, pebble-size nasturtium seeds. The smallest seeds need no covering at all; seeds of a manageable size should be planted from 2 to 4 times as deep as their diameter.

Saving seed from your plants. Many annuals, such as marigolds, zinnias, and some varieties of cosmos, produce seeds that can be gathered easily, if the flowers are left to mature on the plant. There's always the temptation, either out of curiosity or frugality, to save these seeds and plant them the following year. There is nothing wrong with this activity, but you should realize that if you plant seeds of hybrid varieties, the next generation of plants probably will not resemble those from which they were gathered. Due to the rather complex laws of heredity, seeds of hybrid annuals are rarely fertile, and if they are, they almost never produce plants resembling their parents. The majority of gardeners find it much easier to buy fresh seeds of a named variety each year, and leave the risky and time-consuming business of seed gathering and breeding to the commercial growers.

Commercial seed growers produce flower seeds on warm, dry, irrigated farms. Their seeds are carefully cleaned and fields are monitored at every step to minimize the plant diseases that can be carried on seed coats. Gardeners who save seed at home can unknowingly build up infestations of diseases that can damage or destroy flowers.

How do I know when to start seeds? The information on the back of seed packets will give you the best clues, but follow this general guideline: Take the number of days it takes for the seed to germinate (given on the seed package) and add 4 to 6 weeks. This will give the plants long enough to develop into sturdy specimens. Then, look on the calendar and figure out about when you want to plant them outdoors. This date will be based on your local weather patterns. If you want to plant outside after the last hard frost, find out from a gardening neighbor, nursery clerk, or gardening encyclopedia the approximate date of the last frost, and count backwards from the total number of weeks needed for germination and seedling growing time. That will be your date to start sowing seeds indoors. If your summer growing season is short, it's always better to start a little earlier than later.

When you are first starting seeds indoors, it's far better to start on a limited scale and have a success than to start with an extensive project and then not have the time or interest to keep it going. Each year you can add to your seed-growing specialties, little by little. And don't forget to label the trays and other containers with the plant names. When seedlings are small it's not easy to tell one variety from another, and it's essential to know which plant is which when it comes time to plant them outdoors.

Commercial seed production is a carefully controlled business that requires a great deal of attentive work—but it is work of the most pleasant kind.

FIVE WAYS TO START SEEDS

Over the years, gardeners have developed favorite ways of starting plants from seeds. The methods we will discuss here are: direct seeding; planting seeds in ready-made peat pots and pellets; the two-step method; using a seed-starting kit with artificial lights and soil-heating units; and lastly, planting in cold frames and hotbeds.

These methods combine different degrees of sophistication and different materials, but they all employ the same principles; namely, providing an environment in which the seeds can readily germinate and grow steadily to a transplantable size.

Direct seeding. Direct seeding—planting seeds directly into the soil where they will grow—is the most basic of all seed-starting methods; it is also the easiest.

The first thing to do is to make sure your soil is adequately prepared. (For instructions on soil conditioning, see page 47.) But be forewarned: even if you have a good-quality garden soil in good condition, it still will not be as fine-textured as the packaged soil mixes recommended for starting seeds indoors. What this means is that the seeds will have a little tougher time germinating and getting going, in addition to having to put up with a more rigorous environment. The percentage of germination won't be as high as indoors (expect around 60 percent), and the gardener has the additional task of distinguishing flower seedlings from weeds.

With these considerations in mind, the process is as easy as walking into the garden, preparing the seed bed, scattering the seeds on the ground or in a straight line, covering them lightly, watering, and then waiting for the little green shoots to poke through.

Because most outdoor seed beds are naturally somewhat heavy and coarse, it's advisable to plant the seeds that need to be covered with soil shallower than you would indoors: no more than ¼ inch deep is sufficient, provided you don't let the bed dry out. Almost invariably, flower seeds will sprout better and faster if covered with sand rather than a garden soil containing clay. Seedlings find it easier to push through sand, and sand also collects heat and transfers it to the seeds better than wet soil.

After planting the seeds, press them into the soil using the flat side of a small board or the back of a hoe. A small board also serves as a "portable path" to walk on, rather than walking over a newly seeded area.

If your soil is not quite what it should be, you can improve germination by filling each planting trench or hole with a small amount of packaged soil mix. This gives you a finer growing medium that holds moisture well, usually contains some nutrients, and won't form a crust over the seeds.

If you sow fine seeds in rows outdoors, sow them on a single layer of tissue paper so that you can see and space them.

Sprinkle the paper with water as soon as you lay it down so it will not blow away. The seeds show up well, and the paper decomposes rapidly in the soil.

DIRECT SEEDING

1. When the soil is ready to work, mix in a quantity of organic matter using a spading fork or power tiller. 2. Make a furrow and space small seeds evenly by rubbing a pinch between your fingers, or, if the seeds are larger, tap them directly from the packet. 3. When the seeds are extremely fine or difficult to see because of their color, lay sheets of tissue paper in the furrow. The tissue will quickly decompose when covered and watered. 4. Using a soft stream of water, thoroughly moisten the new seed bed without disturbing the seeds. 5. Thin seedlings carefully so as not to disturb the roots of the plant left behind. If you thin with a pair of scissors, you can avoid disturbing the roots altogether.

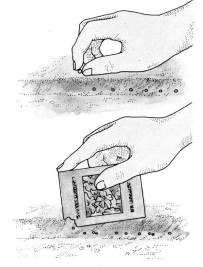

Once they have developed true leaves, be sure to thin the seedlings at the spacing recommended on the seed package. It's best to be ruthless at this stage, because a seedling can't tell the difference between another seedling and a weed—and both act to rob the desired plant of nutrients and space to grow. As with thinning seedlings indoors, it's best to use a pair of scissors to snip off the unwanted plants, rather than to try and pull them out.

The other methods of seeding involve starting them indoors, or in some other controlled environment. Since direct seeding is by far the easiest method of starting seeds, you might wonder why it's not used to the exclusion of the other procedures. Direct seeding with many annual seeds is a matter of choice. Here are some points to consider.

Pros and cons of direct seeding. The advantages of direct seeding include: less handling of seedlings and transplants (once the seeds start to grow, there's no need to move them); tools and equipment needed are minimal; plants seeded where they are to grow are spared transplant shock and tend to grow a little faster than transplanted plants; and the gardener is spared littering the house with pots, trays, lights, and the other paraphernalia of indoor gardening.

Disadvantages of direct seeding include: the process is really only advisable for seeds of a manageable size (minute seeds need the extra attention indoor culture provides); you'll lose more seedlings to the elements,

animals, insects, and inclement weather; and, most importantly, you have to watch your timing rather carefully.

When to plant. With respect to timing your planting, annuals are usually divided into three groups: the hardy, half-hardy, and tender. The hardy annuals can withstand, and in some cases need, cool weather to grow properly. Their seeds can be planted outdoors *before* the soil has thoroughly warmed in spring; the plants can tolerate light frosts. See the list of hardy annuals on page 32.

Half-hardy annuals can be planted immediately after the last frost in spring. The seedlings of half-hardy annuals cannot withstand any frost, so be as sure as you can that the last frost date really is the last frost of the season by waiting a week or so after the "traditional" last frost. In mild-climate areas, half-hardy annuals are well adapted to starting outdoors in late summer for fall and winter bloom. See the list of half-hardy annuals on page 32.

The seeds of tender annuals can only be planted when the soil has thoroughly warmed and all danger of frost is past. If you live in an area with a comparatively short growing season, it may mean that there's not really enough time for direct-seeded tender annuals to grow to a mature size and flower before the first killing frosts in fall. In these climates it's far better to get a jump on the season by starting the seeds indoors, or by buying transplants at the garden center. See the list of tender annuals on page 33.

A SHORTCUT

You can save time and the expense of preparing the entire seed bed if you use soil mix only in the row or planting hole where you plan to plant the seeds. Make the seed furrow or hole at least 3 inches wide and 4 inches deep.

1. Peat planters come in a variety of shapes and sizes and make seed starting a comparatively easy task. 2. After placing the planters in a shallow tray, soak them in water and place 2 or 3 seeds in each planter. 3. Moisture is very important, and it is best to water from below.

Peat planters. The easiest method of starting seeds indoors cuts down on the number of steps involved, but requires buying some commercial products, most of which are made of compressed peat. These peat products are made especially for seed starting. Peat pellets, cubes, and strips (see photographs) are not very expensive and are available at most nurseries and garden centers, and from mail-order garden and seed catalogs.

The only materials needed are the seeds, an appropriate number of peat planters, and some type of waterproof tray. First, read the information on the back of the seed packet; this will tell you how deep to plant the seed, whether or not it needs light or darkness to germinate, and the approximate length of time it takes to germinate.

Arrange the peat planters in the tray and fill the tray with water. If you purchased the compressed type of peat pellet, within a few minutes the pellets will absorb the water and expand into small, self-contained "pots."

The peat moss and other organic materials that comprise the pellets are held in place with a thin plastic netting, easily penetrated by the roots. When it comes time to plant the annuals in the garden, you simply put the rooted plant, pellet and all, into the ground.

After the peat planters have absorbed the water, place 2 or 3 seeds in the small depression in the top of the individual planters, cover (or don't cover) according to the directions on the seed packet, and place the tray where it will receive the warmth and light necessary for the seeds to germinate.

Light and heat. Seeds that do not need to be covered with soil are those that need light to germinate. The light source can be natural sunlight, for as many hours per day as possible; or fluorescent light at the rate of 20 watts per square foot of lighted area, placed 2 to 6 inches from the top of the pellets, left on for 24 hours a day until they sprout. Seeds that sprout best at soil temperatures of 75° F and higher, such as coleus and impatiens, react favorably when light tubes are placed only 2 or 3 inches above the seed.

Seeds that need a covering of soil need darkness for germination. After sowing and moistening this seed, cover the tray with a few layers of newspaper to exclude light, or place flats in a dark closet. Peek under the papers, or in the closet, occasionally. As soon as the first sprouts appear, place the tray under fluorescent lights, or in a spot where they will receive direct sun. Remember, all seeds, covered or not, must be kept evenly moist throughout the germination period.

All seeds need some heat in the soil to germinate, in varying amounts. The soil temperatures needed for germination of individual plants are included in the descriptions found in the Plant Selection Guide, beginning on page 57.

Warmth can be provided by heating cables (available from seed and garden catalogs and some garden centers) or by lights above the seeds. When temperatures higher than the cables can provide are needed, a

piece of clear plastic, formed around the tray and the light like a tent, will hold in the accumulated heat. Another method of providing higher temperatures is to place the plastic-covered tray on top of a refrigerator or freezer; the heat from the motor keeps this spot warm practically 24 hours a day. With either method, be sure to remove the plastic at the first sign of tiny seedlings, and place the tray where it will receive light.

Once the seedlings have emerged, the soil temperature does not have to be as high, and less light is needed. If you have the tray under a 24-hour light unit, cut the lights to 14 hours a day, and raise the unit to about 8 inches above the seedlings. If you are growing them in a windowsill with natural light, no change in the amount of light will be necessary, but remember that the seedlings will grow toward the light source, so turn the tray around every day. On cold nights or stormy days, place an insulating shield between the plants and the cold window panes. A couple of layers of cardboard will work nicely.

Snip off—don't pull—all but the single strongest seedling from each pellet. If you try to pull the unwanted ones out, you may pull them all out simply because their roots are so closely intertwined. Now all you have to do is keep the pellets moist, turn the tray around every day, and watch the seedlings grow. By the time seedlings are a few inches tall and roots have come through the sides of the pellets, it should be time to plant them into the garden.

Hardening off. The final step before planting the seedlings in the garden

is to harden them off. "Hardening off" is a gardening term for gradually acclimatizing the seedlings to the outdoor environment. Remember, up until now they have been growing in very protected surroundings. To place them directly outdoors in the cool spring weather would probably be more than they could tolerate. Place the tray of seedlings outdoors for a few hours each day in a semi-protected spot. Lengthen the amount of time they stay out each day by an hour or so, and by the end of a week's time, they'll be ready for planting outdoors.

When transplanting seedlings started in peat planters into the garden, set the plants deep enough to cover the top of the pellet, cube, or strip with about ½ inch of soil. If the top of the peat planter sticks up above the soil, it will act as a wick and dry out the root ball.

By now, you may be saying, "If that's the easy method, I wonder what the other methods are like." Bear in mind that the quantity of information given here covers also the exceptional cases, the difficult seeds. The majority of all annuals will germinate easily: simply place the seeds in the moistened peat planter and place them in a sunny or lighted location. If you don't want to fool around with providing bottom heat, darkness, or enclosed environments, be sure to check out the seed's germination requirements in the Plant Selection Guide (page 57) before planting them in the garden. For the somewhat finicky or slower-growing kinds, you may be better off buying them started at your nursery or garden center.

4. The entire tray should be placed in a plastic bag to retain heat and moisture. Wire supports can be taped to the tray to keep the bag elevated. The plastic bag aids in the germination process, but it should be removed once the seeds have sprouted. 5. Snip off all but the strongest seedling from each planter. 6. In a few weeks' time, the seedlings will be a few inches tall and ready for planting directly in the garden.

The two-step method: 1. Fill flats with a fine growing medium and dampen. Make small furrows with a ruler and sow seeds. Wrap the flat in plastic to retain moisture and heat, and place in proper location. 2. After the seedlings have sprouted, individually transplant them into small containers. Place the containers in a well-lighted spot until the seedlings are ready to be transplanted into the garden.

The two-step method. In this method, flats, trays, or pots are filled with a growing medium and the seeds are sown closely together; then, after they have germinated and matured a little, they are transplanted into individual containers to give the roots more room to grow.

You can purchase pots, flats, soil mix, and other seed-starting accessories at garden centers and nurseries. Most gardeners, though, augment what's available at the store with "recycled" material at home: plastic containers of all kinds, clay pots, flats, plastic pots, and cell packs left over from previous plant purchases. Foil trays—anything that holds soil—can be used as seed-starting containers provided you can also poke holes into them for drainage. Whatever you decide to use, be sure and keep everything as clean as you can. Use sterile milled sphagnum moss to start seeds in, or use one of the many packaged soil mixes, which are free of disease and weed seeds.

Punch holes for drainage, fill the flats and other containers with the soil mix, wet it thoroughly (warm water helps), and firm it down lightly to form a smooth, even surface. You can scatter the seeds over the surface, or plant them in rows. If you plant in rows, use the edge of a ruler or other straight instrument to make depressions in the soil. Sow the seeds thinly, tapping them out of the packet; or use one of the commercially available mechanical seed sowers for an even spread.

Expert gardeners use an effective material called milled (pulverized) sphagnum moss to cover seeds. It has the ability to greatly reduce losses of seeds and plants by discouraging harmful fungi in the soil. You can order milled sphagnum moss by mail from seed company catalogs. Note: it is *not* the same as the peat moss commonly available in bags or bales.

Follow the instructions for germinating, as given in the peat planter method. Once the seeds have germinated and produced their second set of true leaves (see photographs), they are ready to be transplanted into their own containers. This step requires a little patience and dexterity. A flat, pointed stick (like a small plant label), an old teaspoon or fork, or some similar instrument should be used to separate the seedlings from each other and to ease them from the soil. The packaged soil mixes are quite light and porous, making this an easier task.

Have the new containers filled with moist soil before you start to transplant, and don't let the seedlings dry out between the time you remove them from the flat and the time they are safely in the new containers. Use a light touch even when you firm the soil around the roots of seedlings, because it's easy to squeeze air from the soil, turning the root ball into a soggy, unhealthy medium.

Keep the transplanted seedlings growing in a lighted area until it is time to plant them outdoors. Follow the same hardening off procedure outlined on page 43.

Seed-starting kits. Seed-starting kits are available from many mail-order catalogs. They usually contain all the necessary items—soil mix, small pots, trays, labels, fertilizer, and heating cables—in various combinations. Kits are available for either the peat planter or the two-step method. For the novice these kits are an especially good investment; in subsequent years, however, most gardeners modify the procedure to fit their own needs, and, in effect, assemble their own "kits."

Cold frames and hotbeds. Cold frames and hotbeds are both devices to provide some protection for seedlings outdoors. They are handy in the sense that they take the whole process outdoors, leaving the house free of gardening clutter.

A cold frame is basically a bottomless wooden box placed on the ground and filled with a good quality soil mix. The dimensions of the box are up to the individual, but the sides need not be taller than 8 or 10 inches. The essential part of a cold frame is some type of transparent or semi-transparent cover. In times past, the most common covers were sash windows, and more often than not, the size of the cold frame was dictated by whatever extra windows were available. Windows are still perfectly acceptable covers, but several of the new rigid or film plastic products make unbreakable covers, which are desired by some gardeners.

A cold frame looks similar to a large, covered flat and a small greenhouse. The best placement is close to the house in a location that receives plenty of sun. The cover should be adjustable to admit varying degrees of fresh, cool air. The gardener can start seeds in a cold frame in the same way seeds are started indoors, but it takes a little experimentation to keep the temperature at the right level.

In cold-winter areas, cold frames work best for the early starting of hardy and half-hardy annuals. The temperatures inside a cold frame are usually insufficient to germinate and protect seedlings of the tender annuals.

A hotbed is a variation of a cold frame. The structure of the unit is the same, but before the frame is filled with soil, electric heating cables are installed so that the hotbed can be used in colder weather or during long periods when there is insufficient warmth from the sun. In the old days, hotbeds were heated almost exclusively with fresh horse manure. The soil under the hotbed was dug out to a depth of 24 inches or more and filled with manure. If you've ever built a compost pile, you're aware that organic materials in the process of decomposition give off considerable heat. A 6-inch layer of fine soil was laid over the top of the manure, and the hotbed would stay warm during the winter.

With electric heating units, the temperature in a hotbed is easier to control than a cold frame. Gardeners in extremely cold winter climates find that they get more use out of a hotbed than out of a cold frame, because they are not as dependent on the sun to warm the soil.

Beginners' Mistakes

You should know that you won't get 100 percent germination of all seeds planted, but low, or no germination at all, usually results from letting the soil dry out (even once), or soil temperatures that are too low (which you can check with an inexpensive aquarium thermometer). Often seeds are covered when they shouldn't be, or not when they should. Too much moisture combined with unfavorable temperatures can rot seed. And, in all fairness, once in a while the seed really is at fault.

Leggy seedlings can be caused by lack of sufficient light, too much heat, or any stress that denies a plant its optimum growing conditions.

Yellow seedlings are usually the result of root damage caused by too little or too much moisture or fertilizer. Overcrowding seedlings will also result in yellowing.

A green or whitish fuzz on the soil surface indicates mold growth from too much water, or lack of sufficient air circulation.

"Damping off"—when the seedlings just fall over and die—is caused by soil temperatures too low, or too much moisture in the soil. A fungicide applied as a soil drench (pouring it directly on the soil to "drench" it), before and after the tiny seedlings show, will keep this from happening. Lots of air circulation and somewhat cooler temperatures after the seedlings appear are also good preventive measures.

COLDFRAME

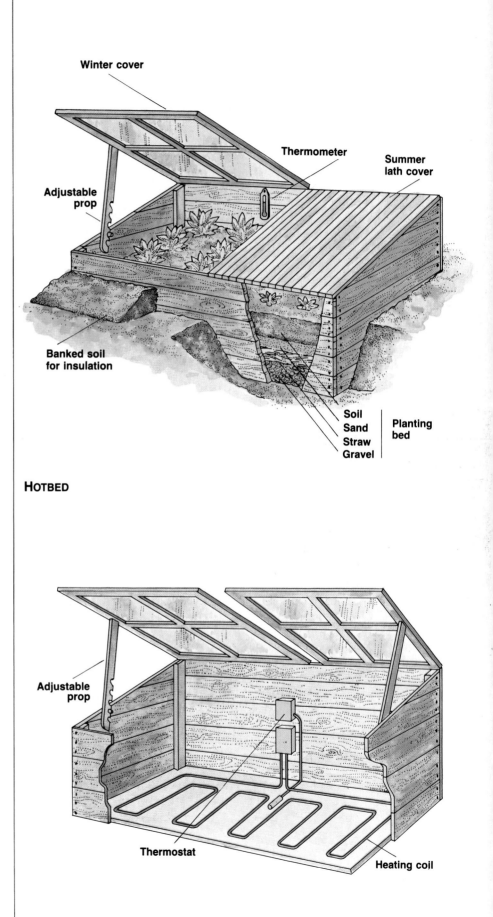

Winter cover

Thermometer

Summer lath cover

Adjustable prop

Banked soil for insulation

Soil
Sand
Straw
Gravel

Planting bed

HOTBED

Adjustable prop

Thermostat

Heating coil

FROM THE GROUND UP

So little care is required to produce so much color and beauty that annuals are like no other group of garden plants. This chapter tells you everything you need to know about growing healthy plants.

Annuals, with only a few exceptions, do not need to be babied by the gardener, and no special or sophisticated equipment is needed to grow them into the most impressive of gardens. Because of their limited needs, annuals are a good starting project for beginning gardeners, and a good way to learn the basics of good gardening.

In this chapter we'll show you everything you need to know about growing annuals, from how to prepare your soil for them, to setting them out in the garden, to caring for them through following maturity. We'll also look at how to pick out the the best transplants at the nursery; highlight some of the common mistakes beginners make; and describe the pests and diseases that occasionally attack annuals and how to control them.

SOIL PREPARATION

The first and most important step is to assess the soil to see what condition it is in and to see if it's ready for your new plants. Almost every garden soil will benefit from the addition of some organic matter incorporated into the top 6 to 9 inches. As easy as annuals are to grow they'll give you much better results if you take a little time to improve the soil.

There's a simple and effective test

An unusual Scottish method for creating a tower of sweet peas. Twigs from last year's trimmings are bundled together into a "teepee" shape; the sweet peas will completely cover the twig trellis within a month or so.

that gardeners have used for generations to tell whether or not the ground is ready to be worked. Take a shovel or cultivator and work the soil up a bit. Then take a handful of the soil, squeeze it in your palm, open your hand, and see what happens. If it holds together for a few seconds and then crumbles apart, not only do you have a good quality soil (known as a *loam* soil) but it has dried out enough from winter rains, and is ready to be planted.

If the soil just sits in your hand in one big clump, either it has a high proportion of clay, or it is still too wet. If you know from past experience that your soil is good—that is, plants grow well in it—there's nothing to do but wait a week or so and hope for dry, warm weather. If you've never gardened in this particular soil before, and you suspect that it is just naturally heavy and clayey, you'll want to add some organic matter to open it up and make it more porous and *friable* (a gardening term for a loose soil of good structure and texture).

Granted, there are major areas of the country with naturally occurring "good soil" that requires little attention from the gardener. If you are one of these fortunate people, consider yourself blessed, because there's nothing quite like having a good-quality soil to garden in. But if you're not so fortunate, don't even consider trying to garden in soil that hasn't been improved in some way. There's nothing that will dampen the enthusiasm of a beginning gardener more than having to deal with a difficult soil that produces minimum success and plenty of problems.

The gardens that produce the best results are almost always those where the owner has taken a few extra steps to ensure success from the beginning. From bottom to top: red-violet and pink stock, white, pink, and lavender china asters. Towering in the background are white and pink cosmos and yellow coreopsis.

When you add organic soil amendments to your garden soil, don't skimp. Many products are available to choose from, including compost, sawdust, and the gardener's old stand-by, manure. Below: Soil test kits are easy for the home gardener to use and are available at most nurseries and garden supply centers.

Improving the soil. Improving a soil with either too much clay or sand in it is an easy task that need only be repeated once a year. The old gardener's secret is organic matter—and plenty of it—incorporated into the top layer of soil. The organic matter you choose can be any one of a number of commercially available products, such as peat moss, manure, sawdust, or ground bark, or a homemade product like compost or shredded leaves.

The addition of quantities of organic matter provides three benefits to problem soils: it opens up fine-textured soils; it improves drainage; and it allows air to move more readily through the soil, thus warming it up earlier in the spring and also providing oxygen for plant roots.

Adobe or heavy clay soil is often better gardened "on" rather than "in." So much organic matter is required to change it significantly that gardeners frequently choose to build raised beds of good soil instead.

In lighter, more coarse-textured, sandy soils, organic matter traps moisture and nutrients in the root zone. Sandy soil has a limitless appetite for organic matter—the more you add, the more you increase the soil's capacity to hold moisture and nutrients.

How much organic matter should you add? Enough to change the physical structure of the soil. This means that at least a third of the final mix should be organic matter. If you spread at least a 2-inch-thick layer of organic matter over the soil and work it in to a depth of 6 inches (using a shovel or a rototiller) you will have the correct proportions. If you intend to cultivate to a deeper level, add proportionately more soil amendment.

There is no point in being stingy at this stage: small amounts of any amendment won't change the soil structure; so be sure and spread the organic matter around with a free hand. If it's peat moss you intend to use, be sure to moisten it first with warm water (while it's still in the bag) or use a "wetting agent," available at garden centers and especially made for this purpose. And take note: *the yearly addition of organic matter to your soil will eventually result in the best garden soil possible.*

Acidity and Alkalinity

One soil test that may be well worth your making is a pH test, which measures acidity and alkalinity. Many states offer free or low-cost pH tests (for details, call your County Extension Agent); or, you likely will find inexpensive testing kits at your local garden center. The test is easy.

The pH scale runs from 0 to 14, with 7 the neutral level. Soils that read less than 7 are on the acid side, those higher on the alkaline side. Soil pH is important because it affects soil chemistry and plant metabolism. Most plants will perform well in soils that test between 6.1 and 7.5 pH. There are optimum ranges, however, within which certain plants thrive.

The recommended optimum pH for annuals is between 6.5 and 6.8. If your soil varies widely above or below

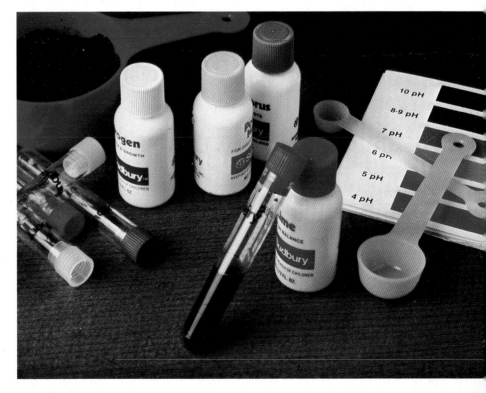

that range, you will want to adjust it. You can lower your soil pH by adding soil sulfur or acid-forming mulch, or raise it by adding lime, in the recommended amounts.

For more information, see your County Extension Agent or local nurseryman. And for a complete discussion of pH and how it affects plants, see Ortho's *Fertilizers, Soils & Water*.

Working the Soil

If your soil test indicated that your soil was ready to be planted, or if you've just added a layer of organic matter over the top of the soil to improve its quality, the next step is to "work" the soil. This means different things to different gardeners: some use a shovel or digging fork to turn the top layer over, breaking it up into small particles as they go. Those with at least fairly large gardens use a rototiller to cultivate the soil. If you use a rototiller, don't overdo it; a couple of passes should make a good seed or planting bed; any more than that will make the soil texture so fine that the first application of water will result in a nearly impenetrable crust.

Many gardeners make a regular practice of spreading 3 to 5 pounds of a 5–10–5 (or similar balance) fertilizer per 100 square feet of area on the ground before cultivating to get the plants off to a good start. Organic gardeners can spread a light dressing of poultry or sheep manure and work it in.

After you have finished working the soil, use a metal rake to smooth the surface, and then get ready to start planting.

A Visit to the Garden Center

You can learn a great deal about annuals just by taking a trip to your local nursery or garden center. It's one thing to read about certain plants and look at photographs in books and catalogs, but it's another thing altogether to be able to see the actual plants. Look around and you'll probably see a wide variety of seeds, displayed in racks, from several seed companies. You likely will also see an assortment of annuals in various states of maturity in cell packs, flats, 4-inch pots, and maybe even 1-gallon cans or 8-inch pots.

The order in which we have described annuals in the nursery, from seed to gallon cans, is probably also the order of the cost of the individual plants—from the least expensive to the most. Generally speaking, the larger the size of the plant, the more it will cost.

Left: For most average-size gardens, hand-digging with a shovel or spade is the easiest way to cultivate a bed or border. Below: Annuals are available in a variety of forms, including seed packets, plastic six packs, 4-inch pots, and 6-inch pots.

Most garden centers offer an impressive selection of annuals in every stage of development—from seed packets to plants in bloom.

But even the largest annuals will be among the least expensive plants in the nursery when compared with trees, shrubs, and perennials. Although they are temporary plants, annuals represent a good value to gardeners looking for a big effect on a small budget.

If you'd rather leave the starting of seeds to the commercial grower, then go with the already started transplants. Choose plants with compact foliage and good leaf color. It's a temptation, we know, to pick out plants in bloom, but younger plants usually give more satisfactory results in the long run. Annuals in bud or sparse bloom are fine, but avoid leggy or heavy-blooming ones. Also, fresh stock is always preferable to plants that have been held for a number of weeks. It's a good idea to inquire as to the dates that the nursery receives its shipment from the wholesale grower. If you're at the nursery when the truck is unloaded, not only will you get the freshest plants, but you'll also be able to pick from the widest selection of plants carried by that nursery.

Once you have selected your transplants, if you don't get around to planting all of them in one day, be sure and keep them well watered until you do. There's not much room for water in those small containers, and it doesn't take long for them to dry out.

Annuals in 4-inch pots or 1-gallon cans may not be the least expensive way to garden, but they're great for those who want instant color, or something to slip into a pot for an immediate effect.

GETTING THEM IN THE GROUND

Every year there are special days that people who love to grow things wait for. Marked not on any calendar, but in the hearts of gardeners everywhere, these days are as distinct and special as Easter or Thanksgiving. On certain days in early spring, the sun shines sweetly, the birds sing, and the slowly warming soil lies waiting to be worked. Anyone who's ever had good garden dirt under his or her nails finds it difficult to resist the temptation to get out of doors, armed with a shovel and a trowel, to plant yet another garden filled with promise and surprise.

By now you have already purchased transplants of the annuals you want to grow at the garden center or nursery, or have the transplants you started from seed hardened off (see page 43) and ready for the garden.

Transplanting into the garden. Whenever you transplant seedlings or any nursery stock, keep these following points in mind:
►Have the planting bed prepared and watered ahead of time; pick out the youngest, healthiest plants available.

TRANSPLANTING

If you are planting in a straight line, stretch a string between two stakes to guide you. Figure carefully how far apart to dig the planting holes. Dig holes slightly larger than the rootball and water them an hour before planting.

When many plants are grown together in a single flat, their roots intermingle. The individual plants will be damaged less if you pull them apart with your hands rather than using a knife or other sharp instrument.

When planting the transplants, fill in the hole around the roots carefully. Firm the soil slightly with the heel of your hand, and then water. If the soil settles after watering, fill in with loose dry soil.

►Immediately after planting, protect plants from excess heat and wind, and from pests, especially slugs and snails.

►Don't plant dry plants. Water them before removing from any nursery container. A damp root ball will not fall apart or stick to the edge of the container.

►If you are planting from flats, pull the plants gently apart; don't cut them apart with a knife or similar sharp instrument. Don't squeeze the soil or you will compact it and trap the roots inside a tight ball of soil. Plants in packs or containers should be thoroughly watered and allowed to drain for 5 or 10 minutes before you try and take them out, otherwise the soil may crumble away from the roots.

►Remove plants the easy way from cell packs and market packs (see illustration). Just squeeze the bottom of the container in the cell pack to force the root ball above the lip of the pack. Snip off any long, coiled bottom roots with a table knife or fork to direct them outwards of the container the plants are presently growing in, gently taking the plants out—one by one—and planting them in the soil. Plant them slightly deeper than they were in the container, firm the soil lightly around them with your hands, and give them a thorough watering with a watering can or soft-spray nozzle attached to a hose.

By taking the plants out of their containers one by one, you'll avoid problems with the root ball drying out and the plants wilting excessively. Some wilting is natural, immediately after planting, but you can minimize it by planting during the cooler parts of the day (morning or evening) or by planting on overcast days. Wind can sometimes cause more problems than bright sun; protect newly transplanted seedlings with newspaper hoods or commercially available hot-caps for a day or two until they "catch."

FERTILIZER

In general, annuals are fairly undemanding when it comes to fertilizers. Many successful gardens of annuals get by without any fertilizer at all, but conscientious gardeners know that a few well-timed applications of fertilizer will result in healthier, more robust plants and, in most cases, more flowers. Certainly, these are reasons for considering fertilizing.

There are both organic and chemical types of fertilizers. The organic types would include fish emulsion, manure, cottonseed meal, blood meal, bone meal, and activated sludge. When compared with chemical formulations, organic fertilizers tend to be much more expensive for the actual amount of nutrients received, but they tend to be long-lasting, nonburning (when used as directed), and in some instances, add

Gardeners who want instant color and impact don't mind the extra expense of purchasing already blooming annuals in 4- or 6-inch pots.

If transplants are growing in peat pots, tear off the edges of the pot down to the soil line to prevent drying. It's also a good idea to tear off the bottom of the pot to promote root growth. Plant them at the same level as they were in the pots.

For transplants grown in individual plastic pots, tip the pot and tap the plant into your hand—don't pull it out. Plants in six packs should be turned over and pushed out from the bottom with your thumb. Hold the soil in place with your other hand.

After planting, firm the soil slightly with your hands to remove any air pockets. Don't wait for the newly planted annuals to show signs of wilt before watering again. A little extra attention in the first few days after planting will ensure healthy plants.

Cultivate dry fertilizer lightly around established plants. Or add a liquid formulation for a mid-season "pick-up" feeding. Middle: Adding a layer of organic mulch is one of the best things you can do for annuals in the garden. Bottom: A soaker hose conserves water and cuts down on plant diseases.

to the beneficial microorganisms in the soil. Be aware that not all organic fertilizers are complete, that is, they don't contain all the elements necessary for plant growth, so be sure to read the package and know what you are buying.

There are both dry and liquid chemical fertilizers that are quick-acting and safe to use, provided the directions are followed. There are many formulations, but all types of fertilizers list the three main ingredients in the same order. As an example, a bag or bottle might have the numbers "5–10–5" written on the label. The numbers represent the percentages of nitrogen, phosphorus, and potassium, in that order. Nitrogen has a powerful effect on plant growth, stimulating the vegetative parts of the plants (leaves and stems) rather than the flowers or roots. While plants need all of these nutrients, each nutrient tends to stimulate different types of growth. Plants respond to a fertilizer according to the proportionate amounts of nutrients in it. Nitrogen tends to stimulate leafy growth, while phosphorus and potash further flowering, fruiting, and root growth. Fertilizers with a ratio of 1–1–1, 1–2–1, 1–2–2 are best for annuals.

Most fast-growing, short-season annuals can make it through a complete growing season on one application of fertilizer. However, any check in growth caused by insufficient nutrients can reduce the quality of the plant and its blooms, so it's usually better to make more than one application during the growing season, using smaller than the recommended amounts or weaker dilutions. Whenever dry fertilizer is used, follow its application with a good watering. Liquid fertilizer is best applied to a damp (not dry) soil. The need for nitrogen is greater for plants in full sun than for those growing in the shade. As a rule, do not feed impatiens or coleus. Impatiens will form foliage at the expense of blooms and coleus will become too lanky.

Watering

Some flower plants, such as impatiens, recover remarkably from an occasional oversight in watering; others can be set back badly by neglect. For the best results annuals need a constant supply of moisture to provide abundant flowers. A deep soaking is far better than frequent, light applications of water. Deep soakings help plants develop deep, strong root systems, able to withstand some neglect. Frequent light waterings result in a shallow root system, and encourage disease and weed growth. A good rule of thumb is: When you water, water well, and let the soil dry out slightly between waterings. This does not apply, of course, to plants such as moss rose (*Portulaca grandiflora*) that prefer soil on the dry side.

In areas of the country with frequent summer rains, irrigating the garden is not of much concern; but in arid, warm-summer areas watering is crucial. Almost any method of irrigating will work—sprinklers, drip systems, or a patiently held hose—but the best results are often had with a canvas or plastic soaker hose laid in among the plants. This method soaks only the soil, and does a good job without wetting the foliage, which can often foster plant disease organisms.

Mulching

Adding a layer of mulch to the flower garden after the plants are in place is one of the kindest things you can do for yourself and your plants. Mulches conserve moisture, cut down dramatically on weeding, modify the soil temperature, prevent root injury from close cultivation, and improve the structure of the soil and its ability to hold moisture. Obviously, such a valuable aid to plants is worth the time, expense, and effort involved in buying and spreading them around.

Many different materials can be used for a mulch, including: bark, old sawdust, sheet plastic covered with pebbles, peat or sphagnum moss, leaf mold, shredded leaves, pine needles, rotted manure, compost, and rice, almond, or cocoa bean hulls.

With the exception of the plastic and pebbles, mulches have the added advantage of being able to be incorporated into the soil and improving it at the end of the growing season. However, organic matter requires nitrogen to break down, and some mulches that are not completely decayed will, unless fortified, draw nitrogen from the soil, possibly depriving plants. This is why some commercial mulches are labeled "nitrogen-fortified." The home gardener can compensate for undecayed mulches by adding a light amount of nitrogen fertilizer.

Apply organic mulches thick enough (2 to 3 inches) to prevent weed growth. Any weeds that do make it through this layer are much easier to pull than those in exposed soil. Some of the soil amendments are acid in reaction, and some are neutral. Good gardeners find out the pH of their soil and that of the amendments or mulches they add, and add lime accordingly. For more information check with your local Extension Agent or local nursery or garden center.

Whatever mulch you use, pick one that blends in well with its surroundings, even though much of the mulch will be hidden as plants grow.

If you don't mulch, then you'll join those who spend a portion of their garden time cultivating and weeding, chores that a mulch normally eliminates. If you do cultivate, keep the hoe close to your toe; shallow cultivation avoids damaging important surface roots.

PINCHING, STAKING, AND GROOMING

Pinching out annuals when they are young, staking tall-growing annuals, and keeping flowering plants tidy and free of spent blossoms are all important activities. The illustration shows how to best perform these tasks, and when to do them. Remember, an annual lives in order to produce seed for the next generation of plants. All of its energies are directed in the effort of producing flowers that eventually will produce seeds. If you "deadhead"—pick the mature flowers and seed pods from the plant—the plant will produce more flowers in an effort to ultimately produce seeds. This practice keeps annuals in the flowering stage longer, and usually results in a greater number of blossoms.

BEGINNERS' MISTAKES

The most common mistake made by gardeners in general is planting tender transplants out before the climate and soil have warmed sufficiently. It's a good idea to resist those first temptations and wait until the spring season has really arrived, if you want the best results from tender and half-hardy annuals (see pages 32–33 for lists of hardy, half-hardy, and tender annuals, and approximate planting dates). It's important to remember that soil temperature is usually around 10° F lower than the temperature of the air—the weather itself may fool you into planting too early. You can check soil temperatures with a soil thermometer or an inexpensive aquarium thermometer and make sure when to plant.

Another common mistake is skimping on or ignoring completely the job of conditioning soil. Unless you already have good-quality loam, the importance of improving your soil before planting cannot be overstressed. Adding plenty of organic matter as we have just described in this sec-

tion, especially on a yearly basis, can work miracles on even problem soils. All your gardening efforts will be for naught, unless you take this important initial step.

Planting sun-loving annuals in the shade and shade-loving annuals in the sun are common errors. The plants never quite do what they are supposed to and you can't figure out why until, finally, you go back and read the recommendations on the seed packet or in a gardening manual. Read as much as you can about individual annuals before you plant them; you'll be much better equipped to provide for their needs.

Planting plants too close together increases the incidence of disease and inhibits the overall vigor and flowering of the plants. Give the plants enough room to grow to their full size and you'll receive more flowers and fewer problems. It may look a little sparse the first few weeks after planting, but remember, annuals are fast-growing plants.

Failure to get after weeds when they are small causes all kinds of problems in the annual garden. Weeds compete for sunlight, nutrients, and water, robbing the annuals of their rightful share. The larger the weeds are, the more difficult they are to remove, and the more likely you are to use a hoe to remove them. If you have to use a hoe or another sharp-bladed tool, respect the shallow roots of your annuals by chopping out weeds with short, shallow strokes. If you apply a mulch, as described on page 52, many of your weed problems will disappear.

Planting taller-growing varieties of annuals in front of short ones not only deprives you from seeing the short varieties, but also throws the bed or border out of proportion. Granted, there are times when the plant grows larger or smaller than printed estimates, but more often than not it is the result of an oversight on the part of the gardener. The simple remedy is to know what to expect of your plants before you put them in the ground.

Beginning gardeners often complain that they started out too big the first year, and planted more than they could realistically take care of. It's far better to plant a reasonable-size garden the first year or two, and gradually work into larger spaces as your interest and desires expand. This is far better than becoming so overwhelmed by your initial experience that you become reluctant to try it again.

Your checklist of things to avoid should include the common mistakes in caring for seedlings, as well. If you missed these, see page 45.

PINCHING

Pinch out the tips of transplants to get bushier plants with more flowers.

STAKING

Stake tall or willowy plants with small sticks or bamboo poles. Tie loosely with commercially available ties.

GROOMING

Pinch off faded flowers to prevent the formation of seeds and to prolong the blooming period by several weeks.

Gardeners who have taken the time to record their gardening activities attest to the value of a garden diary. Many find it helpful to include the seed packets of the varieties they planted and pictures of the garden as it looked in full bloom.

A GARDEN CALENDAR

Every gardener, no matter how experienced, at some time plans for a certain combination of flowers, only to discover that their blooming periods don't coincide at all: that envisioned lovely mixture of pale green 'Envy' zinnias and 'Imperial Blue' pansies never occurred, because the blossoms missed each other by a month.

In this book we have given you all the sound, basic information you need to grow healthy and beautiful annuals, methods taken from the actual experience of generations of gardeners up to the present and from the discoveries of modern horticulture and technology. If you put them to use in the garden, they will work. What we can't give you, however, is the *detailed* information you need to time your plantings perfectly to produce the flower combinations you want, when you want them.

When flowers bloom and for how long depends upon climate, and climates throughout the country vary enormously. Indeed, they can vary in your own neighborhood. This is why most knowledgeable gardeners today accept climate zone maps only as the most general guides, and always advise looking beyond them to the "microclimate"—the climatic conditions peculiar to your own garden.

The climate information on seed packages, in garden books, or in garden catalogs will help you to successes, but it is at best generalized; and this leaves the job of closely timing your flowers entirely up to you. It can be, especially for the beginning gardener, the one aspect of gardening that brings the most uncertainty and disappointment. But handled correctly, it can be fun, opening up a

whole new world of discovery, and most rewarding, enabling you to truly understand and shape your garden. And this brings us to one of the most valuable of all gardening tools: the garden calendar.

Without some kind of aid, it's virtually impossible to remember the exact blooming times of different flowers from one season to the next. With a garden calendar, however, it's a simple matter to note when you plant certain plants, when they bloom, and for how long they bloom. These notes alone will let you know in succeeding years almost exactly when to start seeds and transplant seedlings and bedding plants, and what to expect from the flowers that grow in your soil.

While the garden calendar is an indispensable aid in creating memorable mixes of flowering annuals, it has many other uses; in fact, they are countless. You can record not only planting dates and times of bloom, but notes on the performance of various plants; on colors, forms, and varieties you especially like and those you find less satisfactory; on fertilizers and soil amendments; on watering and feeding schedules; or on your own experiments with plants and different methods of culture. If you like, you can add notes on nursery and catalog seed sources, cuttings and seeds exchanged with your neighbors, gardening publications, local gardening news and events, and, in short, anything about gardening that excites your interest.

A garden calendar can be as simple as a piece of paper on which you jot down planting dates, or it can take the form of a "journal," recording the day-to-day progress of your garden and your skills. (Note: If your tastes tend toward the elegant, the White Flower Farm "Garden Book" offers a book for garden notes made especially for them in England. Ordering information is available from the White Flower Farm, Litchfield, CT 06759.)

Beyond providing information on your climate and your garden, a garden calendar, by listing the dates you perform certain tasks, can help you better organize those tasks. It can give you a good picture of the time and energy you spend in gardening and how you can best invest them, so that you can adjust your schedule and your expectations accordingly.

All of this will prove invaluable as you and your garden continue to grow from year to year. And an additional benefit of the garden calendar is that it can make good reading and stimulate fond memories during the long winter months, and help you look ahead with even more confidence to the new gardening season.

INSECTS, PESTS, AND DISEASES

Don't let this chart worry you: annuals, are among the most trouble-free plants in the garden. Occasionally, though, trouble does strike, and you should know what to do about it.

A few general things you should remember are: seedlings and small transplants are irresitible to slugs, snails, sowbugs, cutworms, and other insects. Mature plants can survive an occasional attack from these marauders, but unless you apply some controls, it's not unusual for newly planted transplants to totally disappear overnight.

Always favor disease-resistant varieties over others, especially if you've had problems with disease in the past. The information on the seed packet will tell you whether or not the variety has exceptional resistance to specific diseases.

Chemical formulations for the control of insects work in two general ways: one kills the insects on contact, and the other, systemic formulation, is actually absorbed by the plant and kills chewing insects as they eat the leaves. For proper control, you should first know what insect is troubling your plants, and then pick out the product that lists that particular insect on the label.

Most chemical products are available in a liquid form that must be diluted before using, and applied with a hose-end sprayer. If your garden is not very large, or your problems with insects minimal, consider using products pre-mixed and packaged in aerosol cans. They're easy to apply, and there's no worry about disposing of leftover spray.

With all pesticides, the application is half the battle. You must be sure to adequately cover the pests and their hiding places, as the label directs, and don't forget the undersides of leaves.

With any chemical products, be sure and follow all label directions. Don't spray when temperatures are high or when plants are in need of water. The best times to spray are early morning and evening. To avoid drift, spray when there is no wind. Also, refrain from spraying when leaves are wet from dew, rain, or sprinkling, or you'll lose much of the spray's effectiveness.

To cut down on fungus diseases, avoid wetting the foliage of the plants. If this is not possible, water early in the day so that the plants have a chance to dry off before nightfall.

Keep your garden growing strong with the proper cultural care, and you'll have a minimum of problems from pests and diseases.

APHIDS Soft-bodied, green, brown, or reddish insects that suck plant juices. *Symptoms:* clusters of insects on shoots, flower buds or underside of leaves. Foliage and blooms stunted or deformed. Sticky honeydew attracts ants. *Solutions:* Lady beetles feed on aphids. Wipe out infestations with contact sprays such as Diazinon, Malathion, Sevin, or ORTHENE.

BEETLES Beetle larvae eat plant roots. *Symptoms:* Foliage, flowers, and stems are chewed, devoured, or have holes drilled in them. *Solutions:* Pick off beetles by hand or knock them into a can of kerosene and water. Spray with Diazinon, Malathion, or Sevin.

BOTRYTIS BLIGHT (Gray Mold) A fungus disease that overwinters on infected plant parts. It attacks weak and dying foliage, flowers, and especially old, dying flowers. *Symptoms:* Grayish-brown growth on buds and flowers often appears fuzzy. The diseased flowers come apart easily when touched. *Solutions:* Pick off and destroy faded and infected blooms. Spray with fungicides. Read labels for recommendations.

CATERPILLARS Larvae of moths and butterflies that feed on foliage, buds, and flowers. *Symptoms:* flower buds eaten or leaves rolled and tied around the pest and eaten from inside. Most often a problem in spring. *Solutions:* Cut out infested buds and leaves. Apply Diazinon or Sevin.

DAMPING OFF A fungus disease that is most often a problem in damp soil. *Symptoms:* Stems of young seedlings rot at ground level and fall over. Seedlings may also fail to emerge (preemergent damping off). *Solutions:* Do not overwater seedlings. Treat seeds with Captan, Phygon, Spergon, or Thiram.

FUNGUS DISEASES (Including powdery mildew and rust). Spread by wind and splashing water and overwinter on plant debris. *Symptoms:* Powdery mildew is shown by white powdery masses of spores on leaves, shoots, and buds; distorted shoots; or stunted foliage. Rust is shown by yellow dots and light green mottling on upper leaf surface opposite pustules of powdery, rust-colored spores on the lower surface. *Solutions:* For powdery mildew, apply Dinocap or PHALTAN. For rust, apply fungicides as recommended on labels. For both, remove and destroy all infected plant parts and debris.

MITES Minute pests that suck juices from underside of foliage. *Symptoms:* Stippled leaves appear dry; turn brown, red, yellow, or gray; then curl and drop off. Webs may be visible on the underside of leaves. *Solutions:* Clean up trash and weeds in early spring to destroy breeding places. Spray with Kelthane.

THRIPS Tiny, brownish-yellow, winged insects. *Symptoms:* flecked or silver-white streaking and stippling on foliage and flowers. *Solutions:* Cut off and dispose of spent blooms. Apply Diazinon, Malathion, ORTHENE, or Sevin.

VIRUS DISEASES (Including Mosaic and Aster Yellows) Spread by propagation of infected plants, aphids, and sometimes leafhoppers. *Symptoms:* mottling or mosaic patterns on leaves; stunted or distorted growth. *Solutions:* Dispose of entire affected plants. Prevention is the best control.

WHITE FLIES Nymphs are scalelike, flat, oval, pale green, brown, or black, depending on the species. *Symptoms:* Pure white adults are easy to see. Leaves become mottled, may turn yellow and die. *Solutions:* Spray with Diazinon, Malathion, or ORTHENE.

PLANT SELECTION GUIDE

This guide will help you plan and design your garden. Over one hundred annuals are included, with photographs, descriptions, and cultural requirements for each. Select annuals for specific effects, for enticing variety, or to solve particular gardening problems.

Never be afraid to transport your imagination to the homeland of the plants you grow. Few exercises create greater sensitivity to their need and habits, which in the end will produce better plants for you. Picture the South African veldt. Imagine wide open grasslands studded with occasional parched trees and shrubs. Herds of grazing animals crisscross its sandy soils, led by the seasonal ebb and flow of that precious commodity, water. And strewn throughout, like jewels in the desert, or sometimes in great sweeps of color, are some of our most treasured annuals, like the Cape Marigold, *Dimorphotheca sinuata.*

The following guide provides you the native origin of each annual, as well as its important characteristics and cultural needs. Consider it also as a journey through ideas, hopefully to broaden the range of annuals you can choose from, and help you select plants to fit the specific characteristics of *your* garden.

This guide does not attempt to cover all the annuals one could garden with, but does list most of the best. Please note that the abbreviations "H," "HH," and "T" refer to hardy, half-hardy, and tender. (For definitions, see page 6.) "How to Start" ends with a number of days, the time from planting until germination time; and a temperature range, the optimum for germination.

Color and form combine to give this gazania 'Aztec Queen' its outstanding qualities. Right: Included here are marigold, petunia, celosia, zinnia, cleome, and pennisetum. You'll find all of these listed in this guide.

Ageratum houstonianum.
(Floss Flower) HH.

Uses: Edging, bedding, containers.
Color: Blue tinged with lavender or mauve; pure white, pink.
Height: Most newer varieties are compact 4- to 6-inch plants; older varieties can reach 24 inches.
How to Start: For late-summer flowers, sow outdoors in place as soon as the ground is warm. For earlier bloom sow indoors 6 to 8 weeks before the last frost. Cover seeds only lightly as they need some light to germinate. 70–75°, 5–10 days.
Where to Plant: Best in rich, moist, well-drained soil. Full sun. Needs good air circulation. Will tolerate light shade.
Spacing: 6 to 10 inches.
Care: Easy. Water regularly, never allowing leaves to reach the wilting point. Fertilize monthly. Occasional deadheading is required.
Native to: Central and southern Mexico, Guatemala, and British Honduras. Most available cultivars are of hybrid origin.
Blue; clear sky blue, soft steel blue, warm, reddish-tinged blue, cool lavender: ageratum is a treasure chest of this rarest garden color. At one time its soft, downy flowers and open, leggy stems were relegated to the cutting garden; but skillful hybridizing and selection have tamed its form and flowering and made it one

of the most popular annuals in America.
The newer varieties are dwarf, dense, and smothered all summer with wooly puff-ball flowers. The plants display a certain pleasing variation in height, and set close together, create an endearing carpet of color. It has become a favorite for massive beds of blue and for edging borders and walks. But don't hesitate to be creative with these garden carpets: ageratum mixes wonderfully with many other ground-covering annuals, especially soft-textured ones like lacy China pinks or fleecy gold Dahlberg daisies.
Ageratum needs fully warm soil before planting. It tolerates no frost, and the first freezing will turn it a dreadful black. Started indoors in flats well enough in advance, however, it will provide an exceptionally long season of color. Ageratum is not very heat-resistant. In warm-summer climates, spring and fall crops are planted.
You may want to shear dead flowers to help keep plants low and compact and assist their efforts to provide nonstop prolific bloom.

Alcea rosea
(Hollyhock) Biennial, some varieties treated as annuals.

Uses: Rear of the border, background, screen, textural accent, temporary shrub.
Color: Most colors except blue.
Height: 2 to 9 feet.

How to Start: For flowers the first year from seed, purchase varieties specified as "annuals" and sow indoors in February or March. Barely cover seeds, as germination requires light. Set out plants after final frost. 70°, 10–24 days.
Where to Plant: Rich, well-drained soil. Full sun. Good air circulation is best, but avoid exposing to heavy wind.
Care: Water and feed heavily. Spray regularly with fungicide to protect from rust. Deadhead to prevent self-sowing. Tall plants may require staking.
Native to: Central Asia.
Few plants evoke such nostalgia as the towering hollyhock. A favorite since Shakespeare's England, its stately spires of flowers inspire images of country gardens and cottages. Modern science has brought ruffles, doubles, fringes, and flutes to the hollyhock, along with a host of blossom colors and sizes.
Its best use probably remains in the mixed, informal border. Coarse, maple-shape leaves cover the stems from the ground to the flower heads. Its huge size and foliage make it useful as a one-season shrub or a textural accent.
Even varieties sold as annuals must be sown indoors well in advance to ensure flowering the first year. In the mildest climates with a long growing season, you might get a few blooms the first year from

an outdoor sowing. While annual varieties will not grow as tall the first year as they would in their second, many are more resistant to rust disease, an attribute to look for when buying seed.
The hollyhock in Victorian times symbolized fertility, understandable if you've ever fought their prodigious ability to self-sow. While it's tempting to let them go to seed, don't expect the fancy varieties you picked to show up again in a volunteer crop. Hollyhocks do not breed true from seed, and their quality will soon decline.

Amaranthus tricolor
(Jacob's Coat) T.

Uses: Accent, beds, temporary shrub, rear of border, house plant, cut flowers.
Color: Brilliantly multicolored leaves in reds, greens, and golds.
Height: 1½ to 5 feet.
How to Start: Amaranthus is hard to transplant. Direct seeding in warm soil works best. Sow indoors 3 to 4 weeks before planting outside. 70–75°, 10–14 days. After germination, the young plants require nighttime temperatures of at least 60°.
Where to Plant: Any soil, full sun. Tolerates heat, drought well. Indoors, give 80–85° days, 60–65° nights, bright light.
Spacing: 12 to 24 inches.
Care: Do not overwater after established or it will be prone

Amaranthus tricolor 'Flaming Fountain'

Ageratum 'Blue Puffs'

Double-flowered Alcea rosea with Marigolds in the foreground

to root rot. Do not overfertilize or dulling of foliage and stretching of stems may result. Taller plants may require staking.

Native to: India and the Philippines.

It's hard to believe that such blazing color and dependable garden performance can come from a cousin of the lowly pigweed. But few annuals can match amaranthus for height, bold texture, and explosive color all summer long. It is particularly choice for tropical effect near swimming pools or cabanas. Use it for height in the rear of the border, or as a temporary shrub against a foundation. But beware of overdoing it—viewing a large, solid bed of amaranthus can be a numbing experience. Soften the effect by adding other bold-textured but largely green plants, such as the Castor Bean, and modify the texture with airy grasses.

It is especially important not to baby this plant—it begs for a hot, dry location in poor soil and will probably welcome overwatering or overfertilizing by looking miserable, or even by dying.

Amaranthus caudatus (Love Lies Bleeding) is a similarly beautiful relative that differs by having solid red leaves and long, trailing "snakes" of red or gold flowers that can droop clear to the ground.

Either can make a stunning house plant, and there are several cultivars that vary in leaf color and height.

Anchusa capensis
(Summer Forget-Me-Not; Cape Forget-Me-Not) HH.

Uses: Rock gardens, naturalizing, cut flowers.
Color: Brilliant ultramarine blue.
Height: 8 to 18 inches.
How to Start: Sow outdoors after all danger of frost is past, or indoors 6 to 8 weeks before setting out. 68–86°, 14–28 days.
Where to Plant: Infertile soil with sharp drainage. Full sun.
Spacing: 10 to 12 inches.
Care: Feed little, if any. Cut back to 6 inches high after first bloom.
Native to: South Africa.

Anchusa capensis produces some of the most vivid, cleanest blues in the plant kingdom, rivaling even delphiniums and lobelia for color intensity. The individual flowers are tiny and borne in great clouds atop 12- to 18-inch stems. Unfortunately, the rather coarse foliage and top-heavy branching limits its versatility, and it is best to hide these undesirable features within the mixed border. Most varieties eventually reach 12 or 18 inches high, but some of the best color selections are, happily, also more compact, 8 to 10 inches. These smaller cultivars make outstanding solid-blue beds.

Anchusa is not a difficult plant to grow, and requires little special treatment. Shear the plants back a bit after each wave of bloom, and you can expect multitudinous blue from June to frost.

Antirrhinum majus
(Snapdragon) HH.

Uses: Beds, borders, cut flowers. Dwarf types excellent for edging and massed beds; tallest for rear of the border.
Color: Wide range from maroon to white, including reds, pinks, yellow, orange, and bronze.
Height: 6 inches to 4 feet. Generally sold as small, or dwarf (6 to 9 inches), medium (18 to 24 inches), and tall (36 to 48 inches).
How to Start: For best results, sow indoors 6 to 8 weeks before setting out after the last frost. Can be sown in the ground after it warms. Do not cover seeds, as light is required for germination. 70°, 10–14 days.
Where to Plant: Rich, well-drained, neutral to alkaline soil high in organic matter. Full sun. Tolerates heat well.
Spacing: 6 to 12 inches.
Care: Fertilize once a month and water moderately. Pinch young plants for heavier branching and better flowering. Will die out if seed heads are not sheared off. Remove spent blossoms to improve bloom. Plant rust-resistant varieties or expect to use fungicide regularly to prevent rust and mildew. Taller varieties will require staking.
Native to: The Mediterranean region.

The snapdragon's crisp, tapering spikes are, happily, one of the most familiar sights in American gardens. Nearly

Antirrhinum majus
'Spring Giant Red'

Antirrhinum majus **'Pixie Pink'**

Anchusa capensis **'Blue Angel'**

every child has delighted in squeezing the flowers, which then open like the jaws of some fantastic creature. Their soft, pastel yellows and pinks, warm reds, burgundies, or bronzes are abundant from May to frost. Varied form and size give them outstanding versatility in borders and beds. The tallest are indispensable for massing in the rear of the border and for cutting for arrangements. The medium-size varieties blend beautifully into the middle range of the mixed border. Use them here and there as vertical accents among rounded or low-growing annuals or mass them in undulating waves. The low, spreading dwarf cultivars make neat edges to the border or excellent solid beds of color.

Snapdragons self-sow abundantly, yet are seldom intrusive. Their ability to pop up in the most unexpected places can be a delightful bonus for the gardener. Pinching, difficult for some tenderhearted folk, is absolutely necessary for well-developed, free-flowering plants.

Arctotis stoechadifolia var. grandis and hybrids
(African Daisy) T.

Uses: Borders and beds. Possibly cut flowers, although flowers close at night.

Color: Petals creamy white above, purplish below, with a dark lavender center. Hybrids are brilliant yellow, white, pink, bronze, red, and orange.

Height: To 30 inches, but hybrids are usually only 10 to 12 inches.

How to Start: Can sow outside in early spring, but best to sow indoors 6 to 8 weeks before last frost. 55–70°, 20–30 days. Use fresh seed, as it degenerates quickly when stored.

Where to Plant: Light sandy loam, full sun. Best where summer nights are cool. Withstands drought well.

Spacing: 12 inches.

Care: Water, fertilize infrequently. Remove faded blossoms to prolong bloom.

Native to: South Africa.

One usually associates daisylike flowers, particularly those of African origin, with a feeling of intense heat—bright, warm colors in a sunlike shape. The African daisy, however, is surprisingly "cool" in appearance, having pale white petals with an almost imperceptible lavender blush surrounding a pastel blue eye. The petal undersides—quite evident when the flowers close early in the evening and on cloudy days—are lavender blue. Standing tall above bushy mounds of whitish, hairy leaves, these flowers seem cool and fresh on the sunniest, hottest days. The many annual hybrids of arctotis, however, are available in a wide range of warm, bright colors. They also grow lower, rarely exceeding 10 or 12 inches in height.

All arctotis have a preference for the rich, sandy soil, full sun, and mild summer nights one would expect from a South African native. It combines well with other daisylike

South African plants: a bed of African daisies, gazanias, and gerberas can be a stunning sight on a bright day.

Don't let the phrase "tender annual" fool you, as this plant is quite tough when it comes to poor soil and drought.

Begonia × semperflorens-cultorum
(Wax Begonia; Fibrous-rooted Begonia) HH.

Uses: Edging, bedding, borders, indoor plant, and containers.

Color: Flowers in shades of pink, white, and red. Foliage green, bronze, mahogany with a reddish tint, or variegated green and white.

Height: 6 to 12 inches; a few varieties reach 16 inches.

How to Start: Sow seeds 12 to 14 weeks before planting out after the last frost. The very fine, powdery seeds need light to germinate, so do not cover with soil. Propagate also by leaf or softwood cuttings. 70–75°, 15–20 days.

Where to Plant: Rich, well-drained soil, light shade. (Hybrids tolerate full sun in cool-summer climates.) Indoors, give them 65° nights and 75–85° days, in an east window in summer and a south window in winter.

Spacing: 8 to 10 inches apart.

Care: Allow soil to dry out between waterings. Fertilize heavily. Dig and bring indoors for winter.

Native to: Of hybrid origin. Parents native to the tropics and subtropics of South America.

Begonias call to mind the lavishness of Victorian estate gardening. Such gardening at the turn of the century was marked with a taste for the exotic and curious, with the ability to support hothouses, and with the new-found glory of scientific hybridization. All three seemed to be epitomized in the begonia, and the fibrous-rooted annuals of this genus quickly became one of the most important plants for bedding and edging, particularly in the shade.

And yet, unlike many other annuals of that era, begonias have, if anything, increased in popularity. Blessed with a wide range of modern attributes, including an easy nature tolerant of abuse, nearly equal adaptability to sun or shade, a compact, floriferous habit, wide variety in form and flower shape, a long-season effectiveness, and the dual attraction of both colorful foliage and flowers, the wax begonia has become one of the top ten most popular bedding plants in America.

Begonias are easy to grow from seed, although the process is long and requires patience. Sow the fine, dustlike seeds as thinly as possible on a flat of moist sand, or peat mixed with sand. The exposed seeds dry out quickly, so cover the flat with a sheet of glass to provide high humidity. Keep the medium moist by soaking up water from the bottom.

Arctotis hybrids, mixed colors

***Begonia* × *semperflorens-cultorum* 'Linda'**

As soon as the seeds sprout, raise the glass cover gradually, day by day, to increase air circulation. After 8 weeks transfer the young plants to another flat of potting soil. Plant them outside 3 or 4 weeks later, as soon as all danger of frost has passed. Many people choose the more quickly gratifying method of purchasing young plants from the nursery.

Begonias are excellent for bedding and edging in light to medium shade. They also perform well in full sun as long as summers are relatively cool (not exceeding 90°).

Hybridizers have had a field day with begonias, and a profuse array of new varieties appears yearly. All bear glossy, waxy leaves and flowers from May until frost.

Brachycome iberidifolia
(Swan River Daisy) HH.

Uses: Edging, rock gardens, cut flowers, containers.
Color: Blue, rose, white, or violet, with dark centers.
Height: 10 to 16 inches.
How to Start: Sow indoors 4 to 6 weeks prior to last frost. 60–70°, 10–18 days.
Where to Plant: Prefers cool summers, rich, well-drained, moist soil, full sun.
Spacing: 6 inches.
Care: Short bloom season: best to provide successive plantings three weeks apart to assure continual bloom. Declines and thins as summer heat mounts.

Native to: Australia.

The swan river daisy is a little-known charmer, but if you're fortunate enough to locate seed, its delightfully fragrant, profuse flowers, held above wispy, feathery foliage, are certain to please.

The plant's decline with summer heat may contribute to its "lesser-known" status, although many of the more popular annuals behave similarly. Try it in the mixed border, where later-blooming annuals can hide it as it fades. If you like cut flowers, successive plantings will provide fragrant blooms all season.

Brassica oleracea acephala
(Flowering Kale) H.
Brassica oleracea capitata
(Ornamental Cabbage) H.

Uses: Bedding, carpet and pattern beds, pot plant, specimen.
Color: Foliage is composed of thick, blue-green leaves with centers of white, pink, red, magenta, or purple.
Height: 10 to 15 inches.
How to Start: Sow indoors 6 to 8 weeks before setting out in February or March for spring display, or June and July for fall and winter effect. Ornamental cabbage seed should be sown and chilled in refrigerator for 3 days, then kept at 65–70° until germination takes place. Light is required, so don't cover seeds. Flowering kale seed requires neither chilling nor light to germinate. After germination, both should

be grown at 60° for 3 to 4 weeks, then hardened off for a week before being placed outside.
Where to Plant: Moist, well-drained soil and full sun. Flowering kale performs better and more colorfully if grown in the cooler temperatures of fall.
Spacing: 15 to 20 inches.
Care: Easy. Keep soil evenly moist.
Native to: Eurasia.

Flowering kale and ornamental cabbage fit the "horticultural oddity" category, and seldom fail to elicit the most interested conversation. Although often touted as "ornamental edibles," the leaves of ornamental cabbage are tough and bitter enough to defy any tastes. Flowering kale reputedly is edible, but hardly more palatable. And both usually shock the curious cook when their colorful leaves turn deadly gray in boiling water. It's best to keep these plants in the garden.

As cabbage and kale have a tendency to bolt in hot weather, producing inconspicuous flowers at the expense of their colorful foliage, they are regarded as temporary, cool-season annuals. They withstand a few degrees of frost before injury occurs, and in mild-winter regions often remain attractive from fall until spring. Winter crops are spared the cabbage worm, a warm-weather pest.

They are best as fall crops, when their colors have time

to develop fully. Crops for late spring color must be started very early indoors to get large plants for setting in the garden in early spring.

Considered a favorite for pattern bedding (floral clocks, spelling out the school name, and the like), cabbage and kale also make fine, colorful bedding and edging plants. If nothing else, grow a few in pots for the patio. Your neighbors may be amazed.

Browallia speciosa
(Sapphire Flower) T.

Uses: Bedding, containers, hanging baskets, indoor plant.
Color: Dark blue, purple, violet, or white.
Height: 10 to 18 inches.
How to Start: Sow indoors 6 to 8 weeks before planting out after the last frost. Do not cover the seeds, as they require light to germinate. Use softwood cuttings for easy propagation in fall or spring. 70–75°, 14–21 days.
Where to Plant: Rich, well-drained soil. Partial shade is best, but it tolerates full sun with only some fading of flowers. Indoors, grow in indirect bright light in rich soil and temperatures of 70° days, 55° nights.
Spacing: 6 to 10 inches.
Care: Keep soil evenly moist; frequently apply light fertilizer. Cut plants back in fall and bring inside, where they will flower all winter.
Native to: Colombia.

The sapphire flower is another in the exclusive club of

Brachycome iberidifolia

Brassica oleracea capitata, Japanese hybrid

Browallia speciosa 'Heavenly Bells'

shade-tolerant annuals. Still relatively undiscovered by the gardening public, these low-growing jewels deserve wider use. Most varieties will trail, but some are dwarf and compact. Plant them for cool blue carpets under the filtered shade of trees or on the sunny east side of the house. Let them cascade over a wall or trickle from baskets under eaves or lathes. Bring them inside in fall and enjoy blooms all winter long.

The sapphire flower is an easy annual to grow from seed. Start it indoors well ahead of setting it out after the last frost, and enjoy its sparkling, cool colors from May on.

Calendula officinalis
(Pot Marigold) H.

Uses: Border, bedding, cut flowers, containers.
Color: Pure white to ivory, gold, orange, yellow, and peach.
Height: 10 to 24 inches.
How to Start: Sow outdoors in place in spring as soon as the soil is warm, or indoors 4 to 6 weeks before planting outside. A second planting may be made in July or August for fall color, and for winter blooms in mild climates. Fall-grown plants develop larger blossoms; spring-grown stretch in height and run to smaller blossoms when weather grows warm.
Where to Plant: Rich, well-drained, moist soil. Full sun.
Spacing: 10 to 15 inches.

Care: Spray occasionally with fungicide to prevent mildew, a pervasive enemy, and leaf spot. Aphids also may be a problem. Water only early in the day to allow foliage to dry.
Native to: The Mediterranean region.

In historical times the dried yellow flower heads of *Calendula officinalis* were a favorite flavoring for broths, soups, and stews. While the practice is largely forgotten, some cooks may find it fun to try. (Be sure, however, to avoid any plants that have been sprayed.)

Today, the pot marigold is famous for broad expanses of color over a very long season. (Actually, it is not a marigold at all, despite the resemblance.) The large, 3- to 5-inch blossoms can be daisylike and single, or as double as a chrysanthemum. The flowers are borne on strong stems ideal for cutting, especially the taller, 2-foot varieties. Foliage is a clean, attractive dark green. It is hardy enough to stand several degrees below freezing. Two successive plantings, one in spring and one in midsummer, will give you color well into fall. In mild climates it blooms well all winter long.

The pot marigold also performs well in containers, and makes an outstanding and long-lived cut flower. It self-sows readily and in mild climates will naturalize beautifully in the "wild" garden.

Callistephus chinensis
(China Aster) T.

Uses: Bedding, borders, cut flowers.
Color: White, yellow, pink, red, purple, blue, and lavender.
Height: 6 to 36 inches.
How to Start: Sow outdoors in place after last frost, or indoors 6 to 8 weeks before. Constant 70°. 10–20 days.
Where to Plant: Prefers neutral to basic, sandy, moist, fertile soil. Full sun, although tolerant of light shade.
Spacing: 6 to 15 inches.
Care: Keep soil evenly moist. Will not bloom again after flowers are cut, so it is wise to make successive plantings 2 weeks apart. Be sure to select varieties that are resistant to wilt, root rot, and viruses. Spray weekly with insecticide to destroy disease-bearing insects. Do not plant in the same location two years in succession.
Native to: China.

Long, stiff stems bearing large, mum-like flowers have long ranked China asters near the top of the list for the cutting garden. Unfortunately, in the past they have been equally famous for their susceptibility to several frustrating diseases, most notably aster yellows and fusarium wilt. Once again, however, modern science has come to the rescue with the development of several disease-resistant strains. Be sure to select these when purchasing seed or young plants.

The China aster has been extensively bred since the mid-18th century, and many forms are available in a wide range of colors. Flowers can be single or double and in a variety of forms, from pompons and "ostrich plumes" to needle-petaled types. Many sizes are available also, from exceptionally dwarf, almost ball-shape varieties useful for carpet bedding, to tall, strong-stemmed, branching plants reaching 3 feet.

China asters have a comparatively short bloom period of 3 or 4 weeks, and will not re-bloom once the flowers have been cut. If you want them around for awhile, make several successive plantings throughout the season. Try not to grow them in the same place two years in a row, and always watch for wilt. If despite planting resistant varieties you still find a few plants that seem ill, don't waste time trying to "cure" them. Yank them out and destroy them.

Campanula medium
(Canterbury Bells) Biennial.

Uses: Borders, rock gardens, cut flowers.
Color: White, blue, lavender, or pink.
Height: 12 to 36 inches.
How to Start: For flowers the first year, seed must be sown indoors 6 to 8 weeks prior to setting out in late spring. May be sown in July or August outdoors as a biennial. Do not cover tiny seeds, as light is required for germination.

Calendula officinalis

Callistephus chinensis 'Red Mound'

68–86°, 10–14 days. Old-time gardeners customarily sowed seeds in late summer to get small plants in the garden by the onset of winter. They covered these loosely with evergreen trimmings after the soil froze. Seedlings would overwinter and bloom late the next spring.

Where to Plant: Rich, moist, well-drained soil. Full sun, although tolerant of partial shade.

Spacing: 4 to 12 inches.

Care: Easy. Keep soil evenly moist.

Native to: Southern Europe.

Dangling their loose, open clusters of bell-shape flowers atop waving leafy stems, Canterbury bells are perfect for the informal garden where a soft, natural look is desired. Plant them about the rock garden in small groups or across a sunny meadow in a broad swath. Mix them into the cottage garden or mass them in waves in the border. They will behave best planted in dense groups, where they can help support each other's flexible stems. (You may still have to stake them in windy spots.) They bloom from June through July.

Several forms of this biennial are offered as "annual" strains, but even these should be started well in advance to ensure flowering the first year. Many nurseries offer young plants for sale. Canterbury bells likely will reseed, which increases their desirability for some "natural" gardens.

Capsicum annuum

(Ornamental Pepper). Tender annuals, perennial in mild climates. One of the most heat-resistant ornamentals.

Uses: Beds, borders, edging, containers, house plant.

Color: Fruit is the ornament of this plant, in black, red, purple, yellow, orange, and white, often in combination on the same plant.

Height: 10 to 20 inches.

How to Start: Sow seed indoors 6 to 8 weeks prior to planting out after the last frost. Do not cover seeds. For colorful indoor fruits at Christmas, sow on May 1.

Where to Plant: Moist, rich soil high in organic matter. Full sun, but tolerates partial shade.

Spacing: 6 to 12 inches.

Care: Keep soil evenly moist. For indoor Christmas color, grow outside during summer in pots and bring indoors before first frost. Maintain indoor temperatures of 60–65° at night, as high as 80–85° in the daytime, and provide bright direct light.

Native to: Northern South America.

Providing sparkling, cheerful color on tight, dense plants from mid-July to frost, the ornamental pepper is fast becoming one of the top ten favorites for bedding plants. The flowers are inconsequential, but the masses of little bullet-shape peppers start out yellow or white, change to orange and finally turn red, black, or purple. Often all colors appear on the plant at the same time.

Plant them in large beds or use them to edge a border. Outstanding in containers, they can be brought inside in fall for color long past the winter holidays. The bright red fruits are shaped like Christmas tree lights, and are particularly appropriate for that season. Warning: Some seed catalogs describe these peppers as edible; but they have an extremely violent bite.

Catharanthus roseus (Vinca rosea)

(Madagascar Periwinkle) T.

Uses: Hanging baskets, bedding, borders, containers, ground cover, indoor plant.

Color: Pink, mauve, white.

Height: 4 to 18 inches.

How to Start: Sow 12 weeks prior to setting out after last frost. Periwinkle seedlings are very sensitive to overwatering and cold. 70–75°, 14–21 days.

Where to Plant: Any well-drained soil. Sun or partial shade. Very tolerant of heat and humidity, and does not like cool soil. Withstands drought well, although it prefers to be kept moist. Indoors, give it 65–85° daytimes and 55° nights, full sun, and adequate moisture.

Spacing: 12 inches.

Care: Easy. For best results keep soil evenly moist but never soggy. Self-sows readily. Excellent for hot, southern climates.

Native to: Madagascar and India.

For regions where intense,

Catharanthus roseus

Campanula medium

Capsicum annuum 'Aurora'

Celosia cristata **'Jewel Box'**

long summer heat is a limiting factor in gardening, the Madagascar periwinkle is indispensable. Its glossy, deep-green leaves and perky pink or white flowers remain crisp and healthy under temperatures that would wilt nearly any other annual. Plant it as a ground cover, or use it in the front of the border. It makes a great city plant, quite at home in a pot or window box, or draped from a hanging basket, and resisting not only heat and drought, but insects and pollution. Few other annuals offer so much—constant bloom from May to frost; lush, clean foliage; low, neat form—for so little effort.

Celosia cristata
(Cockscomb) T.
Celosia plumosa
(Plume Celosia) T.

Uses: Specimen, containers, edging, borders, cut flowers, dried flowers, bedding.

Color: Bright yellows, orange, red, apricot-orange, pink, and purple.

Height: 6 to 36 inches.

How to Start: Sow outdoors in place as soon as the soil warms, or indoors 4 weeks prior to that date. Fine seed is prone to drying out, but responds to light, so barely cover it. Avoid sowing or setting out too early as cold temperatures (below 60° at night) may cause permanent stunting. 70–75°, 10–15 days. Both plants grow quickly if seeded directly in warm soil. If you buy plants, choose young green seedlings only.

Where to Plant: Appreciates rich, well-drained soil high in organic matter, but tolerates poor dry soil. Full sun.

Spacing: 6 to 12 inches.

Care: Easy. Moderate watering.

Native to: Tropical Africa.

The cockscomb can be divided into two distinct categories that are similar in flower color but entirely different in flower form and appearance. The plume cockscomb displays vertical, feathery flowers that look somewhat like a flame suspended in a moment of time. The crested type have tightly borne, convoluted flowers resembling a rooster's comb. Many cultivars of both types are available, differing in flower color, height, and foliage color (some are variegated). Both types bloom from June to October and make long-lasting and unusual cut flowers that hold their color well when dried. Use the plumosa type mixed in the border or alone massed in beds. The crested type is probably best reserved for an unusual accent or specimen, although it is often found as an edging or in the border. Both are great subjects for the cutting garden.

Centauria cyanus
(Bachelor's Button) H.

Uses: Beds, borders, cut flowers.

Color: Usually blue, some violet, red, pink, or white.

Height: 12 to 36 inches.

How to Start: Sow outdoors in place in early spring or

inside 4 weeks prior to setting out. Constant 65°, 7–14 days.

Where to Plant: Prefers rich, moist soil, but will tolerate poor soil and drought. Full sun.

Spacing: 6 to 12 inches, more for tall varieties.

Care: Water moderately; do not overwater. Taller varieties may need staking. Successive plantings will help extend bloom, although it will decline in hot weather. Spray regularly with fungicide to help prevent rust.

Native to: Southeastern Europe.

The bachelor's button is an old-fashioned favorite for early summer bloom in mixed borders and beds, and for nosegays and bouquets. Its flowers tend to decline in number from midsummer on, but successive plantings can help remedy this problem somewhat. The stems are a bit too flexible and weak for serious flower arranging.

If you choose to mass bachelor's buttons in beds, select lower-growing forms that do not require staking. Always water early in the day and never let them get soggy. As they tend to get ragged and unsightly late in the summer, plan to yank them out and plant a late-blooming annual in July. Bachelor's buttons reseed prolifically and can become a nuisance. Fortunately, the seed heads do attract birds, particularly finches, which helps to keep the self-sowing problem down.

Celosia plumosa **'Forest Fire Improved'**

Centauria cyanus

Cheiranthus cheiri

(Wallflower) Perennial often treated as hardy annual.

Uses: Rock gardens, walls, bedding, borders, cut flowers.
Color: Yellow, orange, bronze, red, or purple.
Height: 12 to 30 inches.
How to Start: Sow outdoors in early spring or indoors 3 to 4 weeks prior to planting out. 55–65°, 5–7 days.
Where to Plant: Needs excellent drainage and soil of average fertility. Full sun or light shade. Performs best in coastal or mountainous areas of cool summers and high humidity.
Spacing: 12 to 15 inches.
Care: Keep soil moist. Do not overfertilize.
Native to: Europe.

Gardeners with cool summers have the perfect weather for wallflowers. Bright green mounds of leaves fairly bubble in spring with spikes of deliciously fragrant flowers. Delightful in bouquets, the wallflower is also a perfect choice to cluster in the rock garden. Poke it into cracks and crevices in dry rock walls and banks. Grow it in the front of the mixed border. Place it near paths or entrances so passersby can enjoy its perfume.

The wallflower will bloom easily the first year from seed, and once established in a place it likes, will keep blooming for years to come. A late-summer sowing will produce earlier flowers the next season. When grown in a pot and placed in a cool (50–60°), bright spot indoors (such as a glassed-in porch), the wallflower will also bloom throughout the winter.

Clarkia hybrids

(Godetia; Rocky Mountain Garland Flower; Farewell-to-Spring) H.

Uses: Bedding, pots and containers, cut flowers.
Color: Shades of pink, purple, red, or white.
Height: 18 to 24 inches.
How to Start: Sow seeds outdoors in place in early spring. Barely cover the fine seeds. Do not attempt to start these plants indoors. Germinates in 5–7 days.
Where to Plant: Soil must have excellent drainage and should be light, sandy, and of low fertility. Clarkia grows well in coastal or high-altitude areas where the nights are cool. Good success, although a shorter season, can also be enjoyed from spring sowing in the plains states. Full sun or light shade.
Spacing: 8 to 10 inches.
Care: Do not overwater; allow to dry out between waterings.
Native to: Coastal and mountainous western United States.

In most catalogs the gardener will find "Clarkia" (Rocky Mountain Garland Flower; Farewell-to-Spring), and "Godetia" (sometimes called Farewell-to-Spring, also), listed as separate flowers. Indeed, they bear little resemblance to one another, and Godetia *was* formerly a distinct genus; but both are now considered hybrids of species from the same genus, *Clarkia.*

Godetias produce clusters of upward-facing cup- or funnel-shape blossoms with contrasting margins and centers. The flowers, 1 to 3 inches wide, resemble azalea blossoms and appear on strong stems ideal for cutting. They are widely grown commercially for cut flowers.

Those flowers usually referred to as *Clarkias* concentrate their showy blossoms in the axils, where branches join the main stem. Their blossoms can be either single or double and look like many tiny ribbons that have been fancifully cut and gathered.

Both clarkias and godetias will perform best, and flower the longest, in regions where the summers are dry and cool. They bloom from summer to frost in optimum climates, for a shorter time where summers are hot and wet. In their native habitat they complete their life cycle on the gradually decreasing moisture from stored winter rain or snow melt. In the South and hot-summer regions of the East and Midwest, the protection of partial shade and successive plantings 30 days apart may help to achieve a longer bloom season.

Both clarkias and godetias are musts for any cutting garden, but they are also excellent choices for large beds, the mixed border, and planter boxes. Their requirement for perfectly drained soil makes them naturals for the rock garden.

Clarkia **hybrid (Godetia)**

Cheiranthus cheiri

Clarkia **hybrid (Clarkia)**

Cleome hasslerana
(Spider Flower) HH.

Uses: Background, cut flowers, beds, borders, temporary shrub.
Color: White, pink, or lavender.
Height: 3 to 6 feet.
How to Start: Sow outdoors in place after last frost, or indoors 4 to 6 weeks prior. Seeds germinate best at 85° days, 70° nights. 10–14 days.
Where to Plant: Not particular about soil. Full sun. Withstands heat and drought well, although will look better with abundant moisture.
Spacing: 1 to 3 feet.
Care: Easy, but water often and thoroughly.
Native to: Southeast Brazil and Argentina.

Graceful clouds of rose and white atop lofty, strong, yet flexible stems make the spider flower one of the most desirable annuals for the garden. Its height, clean foliage, showy flowers, and undemanding nature make it an excellent choice for the rear of the border. The least breeze keeps this plant in motion. Spider flower is most effective when massed in groups: plant large beds for dramatic, long-lasting beauty, or arrange a cluster to act as a temporary shrub. A long-lasting favorite cut flower, it lends an airy elegance to any bouquet. It self-rows prolifically.

Coleus × hybridus
(Coleus) Grown as a tender annual; perennial in greenhouses.

Uses: Bedding, borders, house plant, containers.
Color: Foliage has solid or multiple coloration in many shades of pink, red, bronze, yellow, maroon, green, and chartreuse.
Height: 6 to 36 inches.
How to Start: Sow indoors 6 to 8 weeks prior to planting out after final frost. Don't cover seeds, as they require light to germinate. Easily propagated by cuttings. 70–75°, 10–15 days.
Where to Plant: Moist, well-drained, rich loam. Full sun to shade, although some fading of foliage color may occur in full sun, especially in dry climates.
Spacing: 6 to 18 inches, depending on variety.
Care: Pinch flowers (as they form) and prune stems to keep low and dense. Keep well-watered and protect from sucking insects (aphids, mealybugs, whiteflies) with regular application of insecticide. Indoors, give bright indirect light, 65° nights and up to 85° days.
Native to: Of hybrid origin. Parents native to the Old World Tropics, especially Java and the Philippines.

Coleus offers an incredible diversity of foliage colors, shapes, and sizes. Leaves may be velvety or rough and crinkled, deeply notched or round and full. Easy and versatile, coleus grows nearly everywhere—in bright sun or deep shade, indoors or out—as an edging, in beds, borders, planter boxes and pots. It loves moisture and grows best in cool, filtered shade. If you want to grow them in full sun, try to use only vegetatively propagated plants from the nursery. The seed-grown varieties fade badly, even scorch. Remember that when coleus is grown from seed no two plants will look alike.

Consolida ambigua
(Rocket Larkspur; Annual Delphinium) H.

Uses: Beds, borders, cut flowers, dried flowers.
Color: White, pink, blue, purple.
Height: 2 to 4 feet.
How to Start: Sow outdoors in late summer and protect over winter for earliest bloom; or sow indoors 6 to 8 weeks prior to setting out in cool early spring. Or sow in place early in spring for later summer bloom. 55–65°, 12–30 days.
Where to Plant: Moist, rich, well-drained soil high in organic matter. Full sun. Protect from wind. Prefers slightly alkaline soil, pH 7.0 to 7.5.
Spacing: 8 to 12 inches.
Care: Keep well watered, but avoid getting moisture on foliage or blossoms late in the day. Protect regularly with fungicide and insecticide. Destroy diseased plants immediately. Staking may be required. Remove spent blossoms to encourage longer bloom season.
Native to: The Mediterranean region.

Larkspurs have much the same stately beauty and elegance more commonly attributed to the perennial delphiniums. But, easier to grow than delphiniums, they also enjoy a longer flowering season, often well into September in cooler climates. They will decline rapidly in regions of hot summers, as they are native to the cool, lightly shaded and well-drained slopes of mountains. Mulch these plants well to keep their roots cool. In areas where the spring heats up quickly, set them out in beds prepared the preceding fall, as freshly tilled soil tends to warm up more quickly.

Mass larkspurs into groups of single colors, or plant them in pastel mixtures. The taller varieties make stunning backgrounds to the border, and the tall, strong stems and fern-like foliage are delightful and long-lasting cut flowers. Resist the temptation to plant larkspurs as lone specimens; always use them in clusters and groups.

Convolvulus tricolor
(Dwarf Morning Glory) H.

Uses: Edging, hanging baskets, rock walls, rock gardens, bedding.
Color: Bright royal blue.
Height: 12 inches.
How to Start: Nick the outer coat of the seed, or soak it in warm water for 24 hours before planting. Best sown in place outdoors after final frost. Transplanting is difficult, but may be started indoors 4 to 6 weeks ahead in peat pots. 70–80°, 5–7 days.

**Cleome hasslerana
'Royal Queen Mix'**

Coleus × hybridus 'Fancy Free Mix'

Consolida ambigua

Where to Plant: Best in sandy, well-drained soil low in fertility. Avoid rich, wet soils. Full sun.

Spacing: 8 to 12 inches.

Care: Do not fertilize, as it discourages flowering. Water moderately.

Native to: Southern Europe.

Unlike other annual morning glories (see *Ipomea*), this deserving but seldom-grown annual does not climb. Instead, it sends out many short, prostrate branches that curve up to form a neat mound covered with flowers faintly resembling their climbing cousins. Rarely exceeding a height of 12 inches, with a spread nearly as compact, it is excellent in rock gardens or tucked into a pocket in a rock wall. It makes a neat, colorful edging. Its preference for little water and fertilizer makes it also excellent for pots, baskets, and boxes.

Ipomea leptophylla, the bush morning glory, is similarly bushy but reaches 3 feet in height and width. Its flowers start out pink and gradually change to purple, and it requires the same easy culture.

Coreopsis tinctoria
(Calliopsis) HH.

Uses: Border, edging, bedding, cut flowers, naturalizing.

Color: Yellow, bronze, red, maroon, purple, pink, and bicolors.

Height: 6 to 36 inches.

How to Start: Sow outdoors after final frost in spring. For earlier bloom, sow indoors 6 to 8 weeks prior. 68–75°, 7–10 days.

Where to Plant: Best in light, sandy soil, but tolerant of poor soils. Must have sharp drainage and full sun.

Spacing: 8 to 12 inches.

Care: Water moderately. Taller varieties may need support for best appearance. Removing faded blooms will greatly prolong blooming.

Native to: United States and Canada.

Great fields of wild coreopsis bloom all along highways crossing the southern plains. The flowers of this annual coreopsis wave delicately with every breeze. In regions of extreme weather, however, this can be a problem, as the wispy stems are prone to break in high wind or heavy rain. It is difficult to stake effectively, but fortunately, some lower, denser varieties are available. The dwarf varieties make delightful edging along the border or path.

Blooming all summer long, from May to September, coreopsis is a workhorse in the border or in beds. If the longest possible effect is desired, remove spent blossoms at least once a week.

Like its perennial cousins, this annual dislikes wet soil. It really comes into its own when naturalized in dry meadows, or, if sunny enough, in the "rough" zone between a lawn and a wild place. There it will thrive and breed prolifically if left alone, providing continual color. Coreopsis will show considerable variation when naturalized, including the dwarf varieties; this, however, can lend its own pleasing, natural effect.

Cosmos bipinnatus
(Mexican Aster) HH.
Cosmos sulphureus
(Orange Cosmos) HH.

Uses: Beds, background, cut flowers.

Color: Cosmos bipinnatus, magenta-red, white, pink, and lavender; *C. sulphureous,* gold, yellow, orange.

Height: 18 to 48 inches.

How to Start: Sow directly in place after the last frost, or 5 to 7 weeks prior to that date. 70–80°, 7–10 days.

Where to Plant: Best in dry, infertile soil with sharp drainage. Full sun. Avoid exposure to wind.

Spacing: 8 to 24 inches.

Care: Avoid overwatering. Do not fertilize or flowering will decrease. Need staking, especially *Cosmos bipinnatus.*

Native to: Mexico.

Cosmos sport an abundance of richly colored, daisylike flowers on delicate, airy stems. Unfortunately they are not as dependable as coreopsis.

Cosmos bipinnatus is an open, sprawling, lacy plant that seems to demand staking, but it is done only with difficulty. Stems spring out helter-skelter, and in profusion, each susceptible to breaking from wind or rain. But the lovely flowers in pastel shades of pink, red, white, and lavender are worth the risk. The plant is best reserved for the cutting garden or the rear of the mixed border, where neighboring plants can lend support.

Cosmos sulphureous is somewhat sturdier, although taller varieties also will need support. It bears great clouds of fiery orange-red and golden-yellow flowers on wiry stems that crisscross with neighboring plants.

All but the dwarf forms of these cosmos are poor choices for bedding, where they sprawl and lodge, and are best used in the informal mixed border. Tall varieties make attractive cut flowers, as long as strong stems aren't required. Beware of reseeding. Don't plant them where their promiscuous behavior cannot be tolerated.

Cuphea ignea
(Firecracker Plant; Mexican Cigar Plant) T.

Uses: Rock gardens, edging, bedding, containers, house plant.

Color: Bright red with a black and white tip.

Height: 12 inches.

How to Start: Best to sow indoors 6 to 8 weeks before final frost. Do not cover the seeds as light is required for germination. Constant 70°, 8–10 days.

Where to Plant: Light, well-drained loam. Full sun or light shade. Indoors, give 4 or more hours per day of full sun, and cool nights (50–60 °).

Spacing: 9 to 12 inches.

Care: Keep well watered. Feed lightly every month.

Native to: Mexico.

The tiny flowers of the Mexican cigar plant—firecracker-red tubes tipped with black and white "ash"—with their year-round bloom and easy culture make it a popular in-

Cosmos sulphureus 'Bright Lights'

Coreopsis tinctoria

Cosmos bipinnatus

Cuphea ignea

door pot plant. Less known, however, is its ease and dependable performance in the garden. Mass it in beds or use it as a dainty, colorful edging to borders and walks. The individual flowers are not large. Cuphea displays best in raised beds, crammed close together to concentrate the color. Its small proportions and tolerance of neglect make it also a good performer in the rock garden. In mild climates, it will reseed from year to year, so let it naturalize.

To lengthen the flowering season, start plants in flats or peat pots well ahead of the last frost. The normal flowering season is August. Grow some plants in pots for the patio and indoors, or dig some in the fall and bring them inside, where their crackling colors will brighten winter days.

Cynoglossum amabile

(Chinese Forget-Me-Not) Hardy biennial grown as an annual.

Uses: Rock gardens, bedding, borders.
Color: Blue, pink, or white.
Height: 18 to 24 inches.
How to Start: Sow in early spring as soon as ground can be worked. Or sow indoors 5 to 7 weeks prior. 65–75°, 7–10 days.
Where to Plant: Easy and not particular, but best in full sun and well-drained soil high in organic matter and of average fertility.
Spacing: 8 to 12 inches.
Care: Easy. Moderate watering and occasional light fertilizing will help keep it vigorous.

Native to: Eastern Asia.

While rarely available in pink or white, the usual sky-blue color of Chinese forget-me-not is wonderful to drift through the garden. The delicacy of color belies a tough character, however. The densely borne flowers crown a sturdy stem nearly 2 feet tall. Give it wet soil or dry, cool weather or hot, the Chinese forget-me-not will remain crisply happy. Plant it through the garden in great powder-blue beds, let it flow in rivulets down a rocky bank, scatter it wildly through a meadow, or mix it in informal borders. You can expect it to reseed plentifully and reappear from year to year, sometimes in delightfully unexpected places. Beware of the sticky little seeds, however; they hitchhike to new homes on socks and dogs. The plants are not neat and refined in appearance and are best placed at middle distance from viewing points, where you can see the color but not the plant forms. Don't try cutting these flowers for the vase; they melt away almost immediately.

Dahlia hybrids

(Dahlia) Perennial grown as annual.

Uses: Bedding, borders, cut flowers.
Color: All colors except blue.
Height: 12 to 24 inches.
How to Start: Best to sow indoors 4 to 6 weeks prior to the last frost. Constant 70°, 5–14 days.
Where to Plant: Best in well-drained, fertile, moist soil high

in organic matter. Full sun or light shade. Not heat tolerant, and best in regions of cool summers.
Spacing: 6 to 18 inches.
Care: Regular spraying with fungicide and insecticide is greatly advised. Keep well watered and fertilize heavily and regularly. Taller varieties may need staking. Seed-grown dahlias can also be cultivated as perennials. After frost has killed tops, cut down, dig tubers from plants you especially like and store over winter at 40–50° in a plastic bag with damp peat or vermiculite. Plant tubers in spring after last frost.
Native to: Mexico and Guatemala.

All dahlias are tender perennials whose tuberous roots can be dug in the fall, overwintered in a cool, dark place, and planted again in the spring. An extremely hybridized and varied genus, many are large, towering plants blooming late in the season and are purchased as tubers from nurseries and specialty houses. For a more detailed discussion of this type, consult the Ortho book, *All About Perennials.*

The dwarf kinds, discussed here, bloom well the first year from seed and are useful in beds and the border. All make outstanding cut flowers. Several types of dwarf hybrids exist. Possibly the most popular for bedding are the dwarf 'Rigoletto' and the Mignon hybrids, which produce large 4-inch flowers on compact 15- to

**Dahlia 'Irene Vander Swet'
(Mignon hybrid)**

**Cynoglossum amabile
'Blanche Burpee'**

Dianthus barbatus 'Indian Carpet'

20-inch plants, and the Colt-ness hybrids, which are similar in form but grow a bit larger and more open. Numerous cultivars are available in nearly every color except blue. They bloom steadily from July to frost.

Dahlias are quite variable when grown from seed, with a certain lack of uniformity of height and flower colors. Thus they are usually sold as "mixed" colors in each packet of seed. The parents of these hybrids are native to cool, high-mountain slopes and distinctly appreciate a cool summer. Mulch the soil well around these plants to help keep roots cool.

Dianthus chinensis
(China Pink) H.
Dianthus barbatus
(Sweet William) HH.

Uses: Edging, bedding, containers, cut flowers, rock gardens.
Color: White, pink, salmon, purple, red, or lavender.
Height: 4 to 18 inches.
How to Start: Sow outdoors in place after final frost in spring, or sow indoors 6 to 8 weeks prior. 70°, 5–10 days.
Where to Plant: Best in well-drained alkaline soils with a pH of 7.0 to 7.5. Sun or light shade. Declines under summer heat, although newer hybrids are more heat resistant.
Spacing: 6 to 10 inches.
Care: Easy. Moderate watering.
Native to: Europe and Eastern Asia.

While the common name "pink" truthfully reflects this flower's color range, it actually was coined to describe the form: the saw-toothed edges of the petals appear to have been cut by pinking shears, or "pinked." Hybridizers have capitalized on this virtue by producing the highly frilled and lacy China pinks of today.

Dianthus chinensis, the China pink, forms a dainty, compact clump of grasslike blue-gray leaves. The flowers are largely solitary on many slender gray stems, and are single or double, solid or bicolored, and have slightly or deeply frilled petals.

Dianthus barbatus produces leafy, thick stalks above a basal mat of deep green leaves, each stem topped with a fist of many flowers. The sweet William is actually a biennial, although commonly treated as an annual. And many recent hybrids are in fact truly annual.

Commonly used in beds and the front of the border, the sweet Williams come into their own in an informal, naturalized setting where their tendency to reseed is a delightful bonus. Use China pinks in rock gardens, in pockets of rock walls, or planted in cracks between paving stones. They perform well in pots and containers and make splendid cut flowers for the small vase. *Dianthus chinensis* in particular should have spent flowers removed often and regularly to encourage its long-season, June-to-fall bloom.

Dianthus chinensis is faintly fragrant; *D. barbatus* has a more pronounced, sweet fragrance.

Dimorphotheca sinuata
(Cape Marigold) HH.

Uses: Bedding, borders, possibly cut flowers.
Color: White, orange-yellow, salmon, rose-pink.
Height: 6 to 15 inches.
How to Start: Best sown indoors 4 to 5 weeks before the last frost. 60–70°, 10–15 days.
Where to Plant: Well-drained soil. Full sun. Withstands drought well, but prefers cool summers.
Spacing: 6 to 12 inches.
Care: Do not overwater or overfertilize. Fungicide may be needed, particularly in areas with humid summers and high rainfall.
Native to: The South African veldt.

If you enjoy long, mild, dry summers, an open, breezy spot in full sun, and light, sandy soil, then the cape marigold may be the answer.

If you decide to use this "star of the veldt," don't be stingy. Plant it in large sweeps as a ground cover, or massed in beds. The cape marigold is great for cutting as long as you show off your arrangements in the daytime only. Like *Gazania* and *Arctotis,* the flowers close up at night and on cloudy days.

Most people are surprised to learn that the daisylike flowers of the *Compositae* family, like the cape marigold and so many other annuals, are not single flowers at all. Each "flower" is actually a dense head of many, many tiny flowers, usually of two types. The "petals," if you would pull one off and look closely, are actually tiny individual flowers

called *ray florets.* The "eye" of a daisy is in reality a mass of hundreds of tiny *disk* flowers. The cape marigold bears the unusual distinction of producing not only these two types of flowers, but also two types of seeds. And both will create identical plants.

Cape marigolds often bedazzle winter tourists who see large beds in full bloom in southern California and the warm Southwest. These are planted in August and September.

Over much of the USA and Canada where summers are warm and rainy, spring-planted cape marigold forms rank, lush plants that bloom sparsely.

Dyssodia tenuiloba
(Dahlberg Daisy; Golden Fleece) H.

Uses: Edging, bedding, rock gardens, rock walls, cracks in paving.
Color: Golden yellow.
Height: 4 to 8 inches.
How to Start: Sow in place in late fall, or start indoors 6 to 8 weeks before setting out in spring. 60–70°.
Where to Plant: Any soil with good drainage. Full sun. Tolerates heat well.
Spacing: 4 to 6 inches.
Care: Easy. Avoid overwatering, overfertilizing. Heat and drought tolerant.
Native to: Southwestern Texas and Mexico.

Imagine brilliant flecks of gold over a low, dense carpet

**Dianthus chinensis
'White Lace'**

Dimorphotheca sinuata

Dyssodia tenuiloba

of mossy, emerald green foliage, and you can appreciate the beauty of the Dahlberg daisy. The busy gardener couldn't ask for an easier plant, as long as it is placed where its prolific reseeding is an asset.

The golden fleece, as it is sometimes called, makes a stunning ground cover or bed, and a perfect edging. It is particularly charming planted about the rock garden, in pockets and crevices of rock walls, or among paving stones, where it will pop up year after year in the most delightful places. The Dahlberg daisy is most generous with its flowers and seems always to be in bloom. It's difficult to imagine why this dainty, refined, and versatile plant isn't more well known.

Eschscholzia californica
(California Poppy) H.

Uses: Wild gardens and naturalizing; rock gardens, bedding, borders, containers.
Color: Orange to yellow, scarlet, crimson, salmon, rose, and white.
Height: 12 to 15 inches.
How to Start: Best to sow in place outdoors in early spring. In mild climates sow in fall or winter. Heavy watering until germination will help break seed dormancy. 10–20 days; lowers bloom in 4 to 5 weeks from seed.
Where to Plant: Prefers sandy, alkaline soil with excel-

lent drainage. Full sun, but tolerates partial shade. Tolerates drought and poor, dry soils well.
Spacing: 6 to 8 inches.
Care: Avoid overwatering after seedlings appear. Fertilizing unnecessary. May self-sow in mild climates, where it will act as a perennial.
Native to: California and Oregon.

In good springs after heavy winter rainfall, this state flower of California literally covers the rolling grasslands and semi-desert plains in cheerful golden orange. Modern hybridizers have greatly expanded the color range that accompanies its feathery bluish green foliage, and added double and semidouble blooms.

Gardeners have long been stumped by this plant's seemingly erratic germination, and the answer lies in its natural behavior. If you have mild, wet winters, then autumn sowing is best. Otherwise, sow in early spring and give it plenty of water. Heavy moisture is the key to breaking seed dormancy. Starting seed indoors is not recommended, as transplanting can be difficult.

California poppy performs beautifully in dry, well-drained borders and beds, and is best in informal settings where its reseeding tendency can be tolerated. It is ideal naturalized in meadows and rock gardens, but remember that the offspring probably will not reflect the colors of hybrid parents, but revert to smaller orange or golden yellow flowers.

Euphorbia marginata
(Snow-on-the-Mountain) HH.

Uses: Bedding, borders, massing in difficult, dry soil.
Color: Pure white bracts cover deep green leaves margined with white.
Height: 18 to 24 inches.
How to Start: Sow outdoors in place after last frost, or indoors 6 to 8 weeks prior. 70–75°, 10–15 days.
Where to Plant: Any soil. Full sun or light shade. Tolerates well the poorest soils, heat, and drought.
Spacing: 8 to 12 inches.
Care: Extremely easy. May self-sow invasively, especially in good soils.
Native to: Minnesota to Colorado and Texas.

Did you ever think you'd hear a plant described as *too* easy to grow? Snow-on-the-mountain will grow nearly anywhere in full sun—from cool moist soils to dry, stony banks, without the slightest attention.

The plant is beautiful when sown where it can assert control, such as massed on difficult banks with poor soil. It will crowd out all but the most persistent weeds and grasses. Its fleshy, gray-green leaves have brilliant white margins and the tiny flowers are borne in large, white, leafy bracts. The plant imparts a feeling of coolness most welcome on hot summer days.

Snow-on-the-mountain could be rated excellent for cutting, were it not for its sap. The milky juice exuded from broken stems and leaves can be extremely irritating to the skin, causing rashes and burns, and

actually dangerous if rubbed into the eyes. Weeding out unwanted plants can be quite an unpleasant experience. Be careful to avoid touching the sap if you should decide the risk is worthwhile.

Gaillardia pulchella
(Blanket Flower) HH.

Uses: Borders, containers, cut flowers, bedding.
Color: Yellow, red, or combinations of both.
Height: 10 to 18 inches.
How to Start: Sow outdoors in place after final frost, or indoors 4 to 6 weeks prior. Barely cover seeds, as light is required for germination. 70°, 15–20 days.
Where to Plant: Prefers light, well-drained sandy soil. Will not tolerate heavy clay. Full sun. Tolerates heat, drought, and infertile soil well.
Spacing: 8 to 15 inches.
Care: Do not overwater or overfertilize. Remove faded flowers to prolong bloom. Fungicide applications may be necessary in areas of high humidity and cool temperatures.
Native to: Central and western United States.

Sporting balls of color on leafless stems above deep green leaves, this annual gaillardia finds its homeland in the plains of Oklahoma, Texas, Missouri, Kansas, and Colorado. So think of the short-grass prairies when you plant it, and give it open, breezy full sun and light sandy soil on the alkaline side.

Eschscholzia californica, mixed hybrids

Euphorbia marginata 'Summer Icycle'

Gaillardia pulchella

Gaillardias are a little rough and loose for a formal bed or border, where primness and predictability are required, but they are excellent to mix with other plants in more rustic and natural settings. Place them in small groups at the edge of a lawn, or scatter them about a meadow. Let them peek out here and there from the carefree cottage or country garden. Or mix them loosely in an informal border. Don't plant gaillardias where you intend to water a lot: too much moisture, either in heavy soil or standing on the leaves, is sure to cause problems. They bloom from June to frost. Remember their harsh heritage and don't baby them.

Gazania rigens

(Treasure Flower; Gazania) HH.

Uses: Edging, bedding, ground cover, containers.
Color: Cream, yellow, golden-orange, bronze, pink, or red, often in various combinations.
Height: 6 to 15 inches.
How to Start: Sow outdoors in place after final frost, or indoors 4 to 6 weeks prior. 60–70°, 7–14 days.
Where to Plant: Best in light, sandy, well-drained soil in full sun. Tolerates drought and wind well, and prefers hot summers. Does poorly in heavy soil where summers are warm and wet.
Spacing: 8 to 12 inches.
Care: Do not overwater or overfertilize. While flowers will close at night, you can dig them in fall and pot for indoor winter color. Give it full sun, cool (50–60°) nights, and allow to dry out between waterings. Easy to grow. Perennial in mild climates.
Native to: South Africa.

In the mild-winter climates of the West Coast, gazanias are a popular evergreen ground cover so easy to grow that they're commonly seen as great swaths of brilliant yellow along the highways. They share much in common with *Arctotis* and *Dimorphotheca*. All hail from the balmy, Mediterraneanlike climate of South Africa, where winters are wet and mild, summers warm and dry, soil light and sandy. And all three sport long sturdy stems and daisylike flowers tempting for cutting, but which close at night and in cloudy weather. By all means, use these beautiful flowers in your arrangements, but expect them to show only on bright, sunny days.

Gazanias are outstanding for beds or as a ground cover. Their fuzzy, dandelionlike light-green leaves grow flat against the ground, forming a tight, interlocking mat. White undersides of the leaves add to their interest. They make effective edging and are delightful massed throughout the rock garden or meadow. Especially charming in small groups among stepping stones, or in pockets of a dry wall, they bloom from July to frost.

Gerbera jamesonii

(Transvaal Daisy) Tender perennial sometimes grown as an annual where the soil freezes.

Uses: Cut flowers, bedding.
Color: Unusually clear and intense reds, pinks, salmon, orange, yellow, and white.
Height: 12 to 18 inches.
How to Start: Use fresh seed only. Sow indoors in late winter 14 to 18 weeks prior to setting out after the soil is thoroughly warm (late May in the East). Press the pointed end of the seed into the germinating medium, but do not cover, as germination requires light. It is advisable to wrap flats in clear plastic to retain humidity, and remove it gradually after seedlings appear. 70–75° days, 60–65° nights. 7–20 days.
Where to Plant: Moist well-drained, slightly acid soil rich in organic matter. Full sun, but tolerates light shade. Best grown in areas of long, warm summers and high humidity.
Spacing: 12 to 15 inches.
Care: Keep moist but never soggy, fertilize lightly but regularly. Set the young plants in the ground so that the crown is exactly level with the soil. Crown rot is a common cause of failure. In warm climates where the winter temperatures don't fall below 27°, Gerberas may overwinter. Mulch with 3 to 4 inches of leaves or straw in marginal climates, and guard against snails and slugs. As a perennial, Gerberas are usually short lived, particularly due to crown rot.

Native to: South Africa.
The unusual range of color tone and quality, from electric brilliance to soft, clear pastels, marks *Gerbera jamesonii* as one of the most choice flowers for cutting. Form also plays its part: whether fluffy and double, or starkly single, the flowers, with their long, stiff stems, have an elegant simplicity that fits even the most modern decor.

It would be hard to get too much organic matter into the soil for this plant. A mixture of one-third sand, one-third leaf mold and peat, and one-third rich loam amended with well-rotted manure is ideal. It is critical to use only the freshest seed available, as its viability begins to decline almost immediately after harvest, and reaches near zero after three months.

Few home gardeners outside of mild-winter areas are familiar with *Gerberas*. Where summers are 6 months or less, they need to be started from seed sown indoors in early winter to produce large, budded plants for setting in the garden in late May. Each plant will produce 3 to 10 blossoms that would cost dearly if purchased as cut flowers. The first F_1 hybrid series, 'Mardi Gras', has recently become available. Blooming more prolifically at least 2 weeks earlier, this series will undoubtedly serve to increase the popularity of "the king of the cut flowers."

Gerbera jamesonii

Gazania rigens

Gomphrena globosa
(Globe Amaranth) T.

Uses: Bedding, edging, cut and dried flowers, containers.
Color: Purple, lavender, white, pink, orange, and yellow.
Height: 9 to 30 inches.
How to Start: Soak seeds in water for 3 to 4 days before sowing; to avoid separating the thistlelike seed clusters, sow outdoors in place after last frost, or for earlier blooms sow indoors 6 to 8 weeks prior. Plants will give a long season of bloom in northern states if good-sized transplants are set in the garden after frost danger is past. 65-75°, 14-21 days.
Where to Plant: Best in light, sandy, well-drained soil. Full sun. Tolerates extreme heat, humidity, drought, and wind well.
Spacing: 10 to 15 inches.
Care: Easy. Water moderately; avoid overwatering. Pick flowers before they open fully and hang upside-down to dry.
Native to: Eastern tropics.

The flowers of globe amaranth are famous for their longevity in the vase, and when carefully dried will hold their shape and color indefinitely. Several dwarf varieties recently developed have brought the plant out of the cutting garden. Use these tight, compact forms for edging and bedding where you don't intend to exert much effort. An easy, pest-free plant that fairly demands poor, dry soil and benign neglect, it will survive happily in heat, humidity, drought, wind, and rain, and still keep producing its small (1-inch) round, papery flowerheads.

Remember that the flowers are not overwhelming for the color they bring to the landscape—the ratio of leafy green to flower color is quite large. But for the amount of work they require, gardeners find them a good investment.

Grasses, Ornamental
From the ethereal cloud grass (*Agrostis nebulosa*), to the coarse, reedy, and colorful ornamental corn (*Zea mays* var. *japonica*), grasses provide a variety of textures and colors quite different from any other type of annual plant. In the past, most have been grown only in the cutting garden for their delicate, subtle flowers and seed heads. All cut and dry well and are indispensable for arrangements.

More and more, grasses have been moving out of the cutting garden and into the landscape. Mixed into the border they provide unusual, eye-catching accents. They serve to soften rough textures in surrounding plants. And in naturalized areas, such as the meadow or rock garden, they really come into their own.

Most annual grasses (unless otherwise noted here) can be sown directly in the ground after all danger of frost has passed, or started indoors 3 to 5 weeks ahead. If sown outdoors be sure to carefully mark their location, as the young seedlings ae difficult to distinguish from undesirable grassy weeds. When the seedlings reach 1 or 2 inches, thin them to 6 to 12 inches apart. All of the following annual grasses appreciate well-drained loam of average fertility, and full sun. Keep them well watered.

Agrostis nebulosa (Cloud Grass) is perhaps the most finely textured annual, with misty clouds of white and pale green billowing 8 to 24 inches high in June and July. Thin seedlings to no more than 6 to 8 inches apart. The plant is short lived, so pick flowers before they set seed, unless you want a huge crop the next year. The flowers last long and dry well in arrangements. It is native to Spain.

Avena sterilis (Animated Oats) are tallish, upright, 3-foot plants bearing unique hairy appendages on the flowers that twist about suddenly whenever the humidity changes. The flowers present a relaxed yet bristly appearance. This plant self-sows notoriously and can become quite a nuisance unless heads are picked before they set seed. They are outstanding for arrangements, and dry well. Native to the Mediterranean.

Briza maxima (Quaking Grass) is a 1- to 2-foot-tall, upright, somewhat open grass useful mostly for cut or dried arrangements. The puffy, overlapping scalelike seeds droop at the ends of the stems, and shiver gracefully in the breeze. In the border its greatest effect is in generous massing, as individual plants can appear a little forlorn. It is effective from mid-June to late July, and is native to the Mediterranean.

Coix lacryma-jobi (Job's tears) is a coarse, upright, old-fashioned favorite grown mostly for its seeds. The seeds are dark gray or black, pearl-like, and frequently have been used to make jewelry. The plants grow 3 to 4 feet high, and are effective in the rear of the border. If the seeds are allowed to ripen and fall, Job's tears will self-sow. Soaking the seeds for 24 hours before planting will hasten germination. The plant is native to Southeast Asia.

Eragrostis tef, formerly *E. abyssinica* (Love Grass) is a wide-spreading, arching tuft of narrow leaves that produces slender, gracefully nodding panicles up to 30 inches long. As the season progresses the flowers spread open into very wide blooms, ideal for arranging. Pick the flowers when young. It is native to North Africa.

Lagurus ovatus (Hare's Tail Grass) is an unquestionably popular annual grass, especially for arrangements. The flowers last long, dry well, and are not so delicate or easily shattered as the flowers of many other grasses. They appear atop erect, 10- to 20-inch stems, and resemble cotton balls or rabbits' tails. They are fine for the border, but should be grown in large masses and closely spaced. Hare's tail grass is native to the Mediterranean.

Pennisetum setaceum (Crimson Fountain Grass) is often grown as a perennial in the southern USDA zones 8 to 10. Above zone 8 it will not survive the winter, but makes an outstanding annual grass. The foliage is very narrow and mounded, and effective all season long. In late summer the flowers begin to bloom, 12-

Gomphrena globosa

Briza maxima

inch-long spikes in muted pinks and purples. They do not dry well, as they shatter easily, but are excellent for fresh arrangements. The plant makes a striking accent in the border, and is quite effective in massed displays. Fountain grass is native to Africa.

Rhynchelytrum roseum (Ruby Grass) is also perennial in the Deep South, but grown as an annual elsewhere. It reaches 3 to 4 feet tall, and bears numerous open, airy panicles of the most beautiful shade of rose. The effect is larger but similar to that of cloud grass, and the two blend wonderfully with each other in the border. Ruby grass is best grown in large masses closely planted, and is effective over a long season, from July to October. Use these flowers only for fresh arrangements; they shatter too readily when dried. It is native to South Africa.

Setaria macrostachya (Plains Bristle Grass) is an upright annual bearing narrow, 10-inch, bristly spikes in late summer. The plants are large and of medium texture, growing 3 to 4 feet tall. Plains bristle grass is an excellent choice for the rear of the border, but be sure to group several plants together for an effective statement. The flowers are beautiful in both fresh and dried arrangements. It is native to the southwestern United States.

Zea mays var. *japonica* (Ornamental Corn) can be just the right plant when grouped for that bold, coarse accent. A dwarf variety of the garden

Various annual grasses

type, it grows 2½ to 4 feet tall. Leaves are wide, straplike, and often striped gaily with white, yellow, pink, purple, and green. The varietal appellation *japonica*, meaning "Japanese," is misleading: it is native to tropical America.

Gypsophila elegans
(Annual Baby's Breath) H.

Uses: Rock gardens and walls, border, cut and dried flowers.
Color: Usually white, but also pink, red, and lavender. June to mid-July.
Height: 8 to 24 inches.
How to Start: Sow in place in early to middle spring. Or sow indoors 4 to 5 weeks before setting out in mid-spring. 70–80°, 10–20 days.
Where to Plant: Well-drained, chalky, alkaline soil low in fertility. Full sun. Will not tolerate heavy, soggy soil.
Spacing: 18 to 24 inches.
Care: Do not overfertilize or overwater. For continuous summer bloom make successive plantings 2 weeks apart throughout spring. Tall plants may need support.
Native to: Eastern Europe and the Near East.

Often called chalk plant in England because it prefers limy, alkaline soil, *Gypsophila elegans* is a natural for the rock garden, or planted in the pockets of a dry limestone wall.

A common sight in the flower market, where it is sold as a lacy complement to more spectacular flowers, it can perform the same function in the garden. But the delicate flowers are beautiful in their own right, too, and can be a fine companion to showier flowers in the border. It is particularly charming grown hanging from the side of a wall, and is a prime candidate for growing in the cracks at the edge of stone steps or a dry-set patio.

While the plant is generally smaller than most of its perennial cousins, taller varieties may need support, especially in rough weather. Staking is difficult, and in any case destroys its misty, airy quality. It is better to make or buy wire baskets or cages and place them upside down over the young plants. They will soon grow through and eventually cover the structure. Make successive plantings 2 weeks apart to ensure plentiful flowers, as they only bloom for a month or so. In the mild Mediterraneanlike climates of the West Coast, sowings can be made as late as June for bloom in October and November.

Helianthus annuus
(Sunflower) H.
Helianthus debilis H.
Helianthus giganteus H.

Uses: Background, borders, screens, beds (dwarf varieties), edible seeds, attracting birds.
Color: Most yellow to gold, a few varieties orange or mahogany; all with reddish, purplish, or brown centers.
Height: 2 to 6 feet or more, depending upon variety.
How to Start: Sow outdoors after final frost. Or start indoors 4 to 8 weeks ahead. 68–86°, 10–20 days.

Where to Plant: Any soil, but best in light, well-drained, dry soil. Full sun. Tolerant of heat and drought.
Spacing: 2 to 4 feet.
Care: Easy, but plant attracts many insect pests. Taller varieties will require staking or other support.
Native to: North America.

In July and August, drive across the state line from Missouri to Kansas and you can tell almost immediately that you're in the sunflower state. Golden blooms line the wheatfields, extending across the rolling prairies and into the distance. The range in this genus is enormous, from 2-foot, slender clusters of delicate blooms to the hulking 10-foot giant, *Helianthus giganteus.*

Hybridizers have been busy with sunflowers, promoting many of the common to first-class rank. 'Dwarf Sungold' is a well-behaved bedder with double flowers like mums, growing only to 15 to 24 inches. 'Italian White' is a pure-to-creamy white, an unusual color for this genus. And 'Teddy Bear' is a short, stocky, yet endearing creature with huge, double, furry blooms. The dwarf varieties are stylish enough to use in flower garden backgrounds. The ungainly taller ones are usually grown in waste spaces in the back yard.

Most of the sunflowers still reflect their populist, prairie origins. Coarse foliage and leggy habit keep most at the rear of the border, or mixed in with other more generously clothed annuals. The most common species, from which many of the hybrids are derived, are *Helianthus annuus*, 4 to 6 feet tall with yellow or gold flowers; *Helianthus debilis*, 4 to 5 feet tall with yellow or white flowers; and *Helianthus giganteus*, 9 to 12 feet tall with huge, 12- to 15-inch yellow flowers.

Helichrysum bracteatum
(Strawflower; Everlasting) HH.

Uses: Cut and dried flowers, mixed border.
Color: White, yellow, orange, red, salmon, pink, and purple.
Height: 18 to 36 inches.
How to Start: Can sow in place after last frost, but best to start indoors 4 to 6 weeks ahead. Do not cover seeds, as light is required for germination. 70°, 7–10 days.
Where to Plant: Best in light, well-drained moist soil, slightly alkaline. Full sun. Appreciates long, hot summers.
Spacing: 9 to 12 inches.
Care: Easy. Water only moderately. Plants will need support.
Native to: Australia.

The strawflower is probably the most popular of the everlastings (flowers that can be dried and hold their color). The brightly colored "petals" (actually bracts) of this daisy family member gradually unfurl from a tight-fisted ball to reveal the contrasting inner florets. The dwarf varieties are recommended for beds or borders, but the standard tall sorts stretch into a floppy, leggy openness that requires staking. As such it is probably best reserved for the cutting garden.

Helianthus 'Teddy Bear'

Gypsophila elegans 'Covent Garden'

Helichrysum bracteatum 'Jewellite Mix'

To dry these flowers for arrangements, cut them at the main stem just before the center petals are open. Tie them in small bunches and hang upside down in a dark, well-ventilated place, such as an attic or shed. When completely dry, cut the individual flower stalks from the main stem and thread onto florists' wire. The natural dried stems are too fragile to last. Their form and color will last indefinitely. The Victorians were especially fond of *Helichrysum* and many of the paperweights and glass houses around today still imprison their papery flowers, a dramatic testament to their longevity.

Heliotropium arborescens
(Heliotrope; Cherry Pie). Perennial grown as an annual.

Uses: Border, bedding, containers, indoor plant, cut flowers.
Color: Deep purple.
Height: 18 to 30 inches.
How to Start: Sow indoors 10 to 12 weeks prior to the final frost. Constant 70°, 3–4 weeks.
Where to Plant: Rich, well-drained soil high in organic matter. Full sun. In containers give it light shade. Heliotrope will not tolerate the slightest frost, so be sure to set it out well after all danger of frost has passed.
Spacing: 12 inches.
Care: Water moderately, fertilize regularly. As a house plant it needs cool, 70–75° days and 60° nights, and plenty of air circulation. Keep soil moist and give it indirect, bright light. Easy.
Native to: Peru.

Fragrance is one of the most affecting virtues that a flower can possess, for no other quality is quite as subjective, nor, in many cases, as compelling. The powerful, sweet scent of the heliotrope is a case in point. Some people describe it as vanilla. Others have noticed a hawthorne fragrance, and still others liken it to sliced apples. The British commonly call it the cherry pie plant, claiming it smells just like a pie drawn fresh from the oven. In any case, the fruity perfume justifies its inclusion in any garden.

A favorite way to plant heliotrope is in pots. This will let you place the scent where it can be most enjoyed. And if you can give it cool, 60° nights indoors, it will bloom all winter. As a pot plant it can thrive for several years. Heliotrope is also fine in groups among lighter-color flowers, where the deep purple flowers are darkly attractive. And more plants will provide more perfume.

For old-fashioned nostalgia you can grow it as a standard. The lateral branches are easily removed as the plant develops, which increases the size of the head. Most, however, choose the opposite route and encourage dense, bushy plants (and hence the number of smaller heads) by frequently topping young plants. Don't overwater this plant—fairly dry soil tends to increase the strength of the fragrance.

Iberis amara
(Rocket Candytuft) HH.
Iberis umbellata
(Globe Candytuft) H.

Uses: Rock gardens, edging, beds, cut flowers, borders.
Color: Iberis amara: white; *Iberis umbellata;* mixed colors—red, pink, lavender, mauve, and white. Both bloom from June to frost.
Height: 12 to 18 inches.
How to Start: Sow outdoors in place after last frost, or indoors 6 to 8 weeks prior. 70–80°, 10–15 days.
Where to Plant: Prefers moist, well-drained garden loam; however, it will not develop well in regions of cool summers. Full sun. Tolerates drought, pollution, and heat.
Spacing: 6 to 12 inches.
Care: Allow soil to dry between waterings. Remove faded flowers to prolong bloom.
Native to: Southern Europe to Japan.

That annual Iberis performs so beautifully in carpet and patterns beds sometimes overshadows the plant's natural delicacy. Think of candytuft's natural growth habit when deciding how to use it. A trip to the mountains in central and southern Europe in May or June would find this plant sparkling in small patches, pleasant cushions tucked away between rocks, covered with massive bloom. In these mountains it prefers dry, stony, alkaline soil, which makes it a natural for the rock garden, or tucked into the pockets of a dry rock wall, or patched into a difficult, stony bank. In these more natural settings its tum-bling, mounded, and irregular pattern of growth is especially charming. In formal situations where tidiness is the order, frequent shearing is required to keep it in tow.

Iberis amara, or rocket candytuft, bears white, fragrant, thumb-shape, compact clusters of flowers atop short, erect stems, often in massive profusion. This plant presents a somewhat stiff, candelabralike appearance unless grouped as several plants. Rocket candytuft is most popular in western and gulf states where it is grown for winter and early spring bloom. It is rarely used elsewhere.

Iberis umbellata is bushier with an umbrella shape, bearing flat clusters of unscented flowers in rose, lavender, mauve, or white. Globe candytuft will give gardeners a good show of colors in late spring. Where summers are dry and rather mild, it will come back after shearing; elsewhere it declines in midsummer.

Both plants have many cultivars, some of which are low, flat, and wide-spreading.

Impatiens balsamina
(Balsam) H.

Uses: Bedding, borders, containers.
Color: Red, maroon, purple, pink, white, or mauve.
Height: 12 to 36 inches.
How to Start: Sow outdoors in place after the last frost, or indoors 6 to 8 weeks earlier. Seeds seem to respond to light, so cover very lightly if at all. Keep young plants warm, and do not overwater, as they

Impatiens balsamina

Heliotropium arborescens 'Purple Bonnet'

Iberis umbellata 'Ruffled White'

are subject to damping-off. 70°, 7–14 days.

Where to Plant: Fertile, sandy soil rich in organic matter. Appreciates hot summers. Full sun or light shade.

Spacing: 8 to 18 inches, depending on variety.

Care: Moderately easy. Fertilize and water plentifully. Regular insecticide will maintain appearance.

Native to: Tropical India and China.

Due to the recent introduction of new cultivars, balsam appears to be making a comeback, although not to the extent of the immense popularity it enjoyed in Victorian garden beds. This tropical native produces a multitude of brightly colored flowers resembling small roses, which tightly hug thick, succulent, erect, leafy stems. Two flowering types are available: those that bear flowers close to the main stem where branches join; and those that bear out near the leaf tips. Both are beautiful. Choose to your taste. You can also choose from double- or single-flowered sorts, tall or dwarf.

While related to the important shade-bedder, *Impatiens wallerana*, balsam prefers full sun. In the hottest areas of the South or West, however, it would be wise to give them light shade. For best results, pinch back taller varieties occasionally to promote bushier growth. And you may want to thin out some of the leaves to prevent them from hiding flowers.

Impatiens wallerana

(Impatiens; Buzy Lizzie) Perennial grown as an annual.

Uses: Borders, bedding, under trees and other dense shade, hanging baskets, containers, indoor plant.

Color: White, pink, orange, salmon, red, scarlet, mauve. June to frost.

Height: 6 to 18 inches.

How to Start: Sow indoors 10 to 12 weeks prior to setting outside after last frost. Light is required for germination, so don't cover the seeds. 75°, 14–21 days.

Where to Plant: Well-drained, sandy soil high in organic matter. Partial to deep shade. Tolerates full sun in cool coastal areas.

Spacing: 10 to 15 inches.

Care: Keep soil moist but avoid overwatering and over-fertilizing. Pinch young plants to promote dense growth. Indoors, grow in bright indirect light in rich soil.

Native to: Southeast Africa.

A vigorous, industry-wide breeding program has made this king of the shade bedders exceedingly varied and versatile—from low, ground-hugging, 6-inch types to full, bushy, 30-inch ones, all free-flowering, constantly in bloom from transplanting to frost, and available in a wide color range. Most are solid, intense colors, but a few new varieties are bicolored. Double-flowered varieties are available. Foliage is glossy dark green or bronze.

Impatiens are the best flowering shade plant, both in the ground or in pots. Container-grown plants acclimate well to indoor use, and while not long-lived as house plants they will provide good color until dry air and short days make them just linger until spring.

The ability to tolerate shade is a rare commodity in annuals, so it is understandable that impatiens are used almost exclusively in the shade. Surprising to many is the fact that newer varieties also perform admirably in full sun in the moist coastal or northern regions. In the sun it is vital to keep them watered heavily, and some fading of the more intensely colored flowers can be expected. In desert areas impatiens are hard-pressed to cope with the hot dry air and are usually grown in containers in humid, shady corners.

Due to the succulent stems, impatiens quickly wilt into limp, seemingly dead rags when they dry out. But they will recover almost as quickly when watered. Their rapid recovery to moisture loss tempts some gardeners to use wilting as an indication of need for water, but this is a poor garden practice. Wilting invariably wreaks injury, and the consequent foliage loss may result in open, spindly plants. Try never to let impatiens get to the wilting point.

Ipomea alba
(Moonflower Vine)
Ipomea x multifida
(Cardinal Climber) HH.
Ipomea quamoclit
(Cypress Vine) HH.
Ipomea nil
(Morning Glory Vine) HH.
Ipomea purpurea
(Morning Glory Vine) HH.
Ipomea tricolor
(Morning Glory Vine) HH.

Uses: Screen, trellis, lamppost, mailbox, dead trees, anywhere climbing color is desired.

Color: Ipomea alba: white; *I. × multifida* and *I. quamoclit:* red; *I. nil, I. purpurea, I. tricolor:* blue, purple, red, pink, and white. All from July to frost.

Height: I. alba, 15 feet; *I. × multifida,* 30 feet; *I. quamoclit,* 25 feet; *I. nil, I. purpurea,* and *I. tricolor,* 8 to 10 feet.

How to Start: Nick outer coat of seed or soak 24 hours prior to planting. Best to sow outdoors in place after last frost, as transplanting is difficult. Can sow indoors 4 to 6 weeks ahead, but use individual peat pots. 70–80°, 5–7 days.

Where to Plant: Prefer light, sandy, well-drained soil low in fertility, but will grow almost anywhere. Full sun. Twining vines must have support to wrap around. Tolerant of dry soil.

Spacing: 12 to 24 inches.

Care: Do not fertilize. Water adequately but do not overwater. Tolerates drought well.

Native to: Tropics.

This varied genus is responsible for most, if not all, of the truly valuable annual vines.

**Impatiens wallerana
'Elfin Fuchsia'**

Ipomea × multifida

Ipomea 'Heavenly Blue'

They are twining in habit and climb by coiling their stems and leaf petioles around a support. All are vigorous and fast-growing. Therefore, be sure to provide them tall, strong support early in the season, such as a trellis, net, or nylon string. (Do not, however, interplant them with delicate plants that can be smothered by them.) If you should want to grow the vines up a lamppost or tree trunk, provide suitable "handholds" such as wire or string, as they do not cling well to smooth, vertical, or broad surfaces.

Don't necessarily feel that these vines need to grow up. They are equally at home cascading down over a wall or steep embankment, or from a hanging basket. They can even be used as they grow in nature: clambering prostrate over the ground, up and over large rocks and stumps.

Ipomea alba (formerly *Calonyction aculeatum*) is especially interesting for its large, white, funnel-shape flowers that open at night, releasing abundant, delightful fragrance. Plant this vine on porches and near balconies and patios where its night blooms and fragrance can most be appreciated. The blooming provides considerable drama, as the buds unfurl—usually around 9:00 on summer evenings—to full flower in the space of about 2½ minutes. The large, heart-shape dark green leaves of moonflower vine are a perfect foil for the snow white flowers.

Ipomea quamoclit (formerly *Quamoclit pennata*), the cypress vine, is a vigorous plant of huge proportions—often reaching 25 feet in warm climates—bearing clusters of parasol-shape, bright red flowers 1½ inches across, with threadlike foliage. *Ipomea × multifida* is a similar, even more vigorous plant with ferny but coarser foliage and bearing somewhat larger scarlet flowers with a white throat. Both should be reserved for large areas. They are a bit more touchy about soil than other Ipomeas, and must have excellent drainage with a high proportion of organic matter. In southern states they are often seen twining up porch and carport posts and wrought ironwork.

Ipomea nil, *I. purpurea*, and *I. tricolor* are all sold as the morning glory of commerce, each available in a wide variety of colors. So much interbreeding has occurred that the true original species are seldom encountered. All grow vigorously to 8 to 10 feet, sometimes more, and bear heart-shape leaves that are either hairy or smooth. Morning glories are particularly suited to pot culture, as any restriction of root growth tends to favor more production of flowers than foliage. For the same reason it is wise not to fertilize morning glories. It is essential, however, that they be given sharply drained soil and plenty of moisture during the growing season.

All members of this genus bear ephemeral flowers that last no longer than a day, and even less in periods of intense heat. They begin to produce flowers during July and August, but really come into their own in the cool, fresh weather of late summer and fall. Plan for their greatest effect during that season.

Kochia scoparia forma trichophylla 'Childsii'
(Summer Cypress; Burning Bush) HH.

Uses: Hedge, screen, border, accent, temporary shrub.
Color: Foliage green in summer, tinged with brilliant red in fall.
Height: 2 to 3 feet.
How to Start: Best to sow outdoors after all danger of frost is past. Soak seed in water for 24 hours prior to sowing. Seeds require light to germinate; do not cover. 70–75°, 7–14 days.
Where to Plant: Best in sandy soil with sharp drainage. Full sun. Appreciates heat, tolerates pollution, dry soil. Develops too slowly in mild, cool regions.
Spacing: 18 to 24 inches.
Care: Extremely tough. Will withstand shearing well. Do not overwater. In warm climates cut back or pull out the plants before seeds ripen, as it self-sows vigorously and can become a formidable pest.
Native to: Eurasia.

The summer cypress is another of those annuals whose foliage is the attractive feature. The tiny green flowers are inconspicuous. The upright, rounded, and bushy structure of this plant supports dense, finely textured light green leaves—the effect is like a bright green powderpuff. In cool falls the foliage turns a brilliant red. Use summer cypress wherever you need a quick, temporary hedge or shrubby mass. The pleasant, refined leaf texture makes an outstanding background for beds and borders, and the plant trims easily into formal shapes. Remember its dry soil origins, and give it sharply drained soil and a hot, dry location. Do not allow the plant to ripen seed, especially in warm-winter climates, or you will be fighting unwanted, deep-rooted guests for years to come.

Lathyrus odorata
(Sweet Pea) H.

Uses: Trellis, fence, light post, screen, borders, containers, beds, cut flowers.
Color: Blue, lavender, purple, pink, salmon, red, and white.
Height: Vines to 6 feet or more, bush types to 30 inches.
How to Start: Soak the seed for 24 to 48 hours, or file the seed coat. Sow outdoors in early spring in a bed prepared the preceding fall. In mild climates seed can be sown in the fall. Or start indoors in peat pots 4 to 6 weeks prior to setting out in early spring. 55–65°, 10–14 days.
Where to Plant: Best in fertile, well-drained, slightly alkaline soil, high in organic matter. Full sun.
Spacing: 6 to 12 inches.
Care: Water and fertilize abundantly. Mulch the soil to

Ipomea quamoclit

Kochia scoparium forma trichophylla 'Childsii' with Coleus × hybridus 'Golden Wizard' in the foreground

Lathyrus odorata

Lavatera 'Silver Cup'

keep roots cool. Cut back to encourage denser branching and flowering. Provide support for climbing types. Protect from drying wind.

Native to: Italy.

The sweet pea is almost a textbook case of the tradeoffs involved in plant breeding. The original native, imported to England from Sicily in the late 1600s, was a 6-foot vine bearing pink or purple 1-inch flowers reputed to have been among the most deliciously fragrant in the plant kingdom. Toward the end of the last century, vigorous breeding efforts resulted in an explosion of flower size, color, and form, and in the early 20th century the sweet pea became as popular as petunias are today. Yet the new varieties, although visibly more spectacular, have lost most of their famous scent. Today, perhaps due to this loss, but also to its relatively short bloom season and exacting cultural requirements, the sweet pea has been eclipsed by other easier annuals. This is unfortunate, as it is still one of the most graceful and exquisite of all cut flowers and vining annuals. And recent breeding efforts to regain the pronounced fragrance and produce more heat-tolerance (and thus all-season bloom) hold much promise for its comeback.

In its native habitat, the sweet pea was found growing along cool river banks, in open woods and pastures, and along the coast, where temperatures are mild and cool, air moist and breezy, and sunlight strong. Mild coastal climates where spring is long are ideal for them.

The vines climb by means of short, wiry tendrils, so provide suitable support, such as wire, netting, or string. To produce the largest flowers, you can remove two-thirds of the lateral growth and buds and reduce the number of tendrils to the bare minimum required for support. But this results in rather open plants, and is a practice necessary only for the exhibitor-hobbyist. For a longer blooming season mulch roots to keep them cool and remove all dead blossoms and stalks immediately. Do not grow sweet peas in the same place 2 years in a row. New varieties have greatly widened the sweet pea's appeal today. The 'Galaxy' strain is heat resistant and will bloom all summer if deadheaded religiously. Several new dwarf cultivars do not require staking. And Unwin's of England offers several new strains reported to possess much of this plant's original fragrance.

Lavatera hybrids
(Tree Mallow) H.

Uses: Border, rear of border, low hedge or screen, cut flowers.
Color: Deep pink to white.
Height: 30 to 48 inches.
How to Start: Best to sow outdoors in place in early spring, as it is difficult to transplant. Or sow indoors 6 to 8 weeks ahead in individual peat pots. Mature plants will not bloom after first frost in fall. 70°, 14–21 days.
Where to Plant: Well-drained garden loam of average fertility. Full sun.
Spacing: 18 to 24 inches.
Care: Feed once a month, and keep well watered. Remove faded blossoms to prolong bloom period.
Native to: The Mediterranean region.

This seldom-planted but promising cousin of the hibiscus and hollyhock produces dense, bushy mounds literally covered with flowers in the most beautiful shades of rose and pink. Mysteriously, it is seldom seen in American gardens, although easy to grow. They will provide continuous solid color from July to frost in cool climates. Use them in the mixed border, toward the rear as their height dictates. Plant them in groups as temporary, quick shrubs. Or line them along walks and property lines as a solid pink hedge. The flowers last reasonably long when cut and the stems are strong. Mallows deserve wider use in today's value-conscious gardening, yielding much beauty for the effort required to grow them.

Limonium bonduellii
(Algerian Sea Lavender)
Limonium sinuatum
(Statice; Notchleaf Sea Lavender)
Both half-hardy biennials grown as annuals.

Uses: Cut and dried flowers, border, rock garden.
Color: Limonium bonduellii, yellow; *L. sinuatum,* white, blue, lavender, yellow, pink, and red.
Height: Limonium bonduellii,

Linaria maroccana

Limonium sinuatum 'Kampf's Blue'

24 to 36 inches. *L. sinuatum*, 12 to 30 inches.

How to Start: Can be sown outdoors in place after final frost, but better to sow indoors 8 to 10 weeks ahead. Best to purchase roughened or scarified, cleaned seed. 70°, 15–20 days.

Where to Plant: Best in well-drained, light sandy loam low in fertility. Full sun. Tolerates heat, drought, and salt spray well.

Spacing: 12 to 24 inches.

Care: Water only when dry, as it is prone to root rot.

Native to: The Mediterranean region.

The long-lasting dried flowers of statice are famous for fresh or winter bouquet. But unlike many of the "everlastings," these plants deserve to be brought out of the cutting garden into the bed or border. The flowers are available in a wide range of vivid colors and float gracefully above clumps of dark green leaves. They are exceptional when mixed strategically with other gay colors. Statice's biennial heritage shows in its unpredictable, irregular blooming habits. A rosette of leaves will sometimes sit for weeks while all around it other plants are blooming. For this reason it is seldom massed for bedding, but is scattered among other plants where tardy blooming will go unnoticed.

Statice are an excellent choice for seashore gardens, where they can be grown right up to the water's edge.

To preserve them, cut flowers when fully opened and hang upside down in a cool, dark place to dry.

Linaria maroccana
(Toadflax) H.

Uses: Bedding, rock gardens and walls, naturalizing, edging, cut flowers.

Color: Yellow, blue, red, pink, bronze, orange, and white. Usually available in mixed colors.

Height: 8 to 12 inches.

How to Start: Sow outdoors in place in early spring as soon as the ground thaws. Or sow in fall for late bloom. Can be started indoors 4 to 6 weeks ahead, but this is unnecessary as they develop quickly. 55–60°, 7–14 days.

Where to Plant: Loose, sandy soil with sharp drainage and rich in organic matter. Full sun. Performs best in areas with cool summer nights or as a spring flower in warmer climates.

Spacing: 4 to 6 inches.

Care: Easy. Water only moderately. Responds favorably to light feeding.

Native to: Morocco.

Linaria will bring a festive atmosphere to any garden with its brightly colored mixes. The flowers resemble miniature snapdragons (their "jaws" will even open when pinched) and bloom over an amazingly long period, from April to frost.

Plant them in large beds all to themselves, or as an edging; mix them with other low-growing annuals or scatter over beds of bulbs. Be sure not to let larger plants smother them: they sorely resent a confined space or shade. Dwarf and taller snapdragons are particularly charming to mix with *Linaria*, where the

similarity in flower form and colors is accentuated by variation in size.

Perhaps the best use of all is to naturalize them in random patches throughout the rock garden, in the pocket of a rock wall, or among stepping stones. *Linaria* self-sows readily (indeed, its cousin, *Linaria vulgaris*, is a beautiful but invasive weed in the East), and should be planted where this is not a problem. A meadow garden is ideal.

Linaria is an exceptionally easy and productive plant that should be used more often.

Lobelia erinus
(Edging Lobelia) HH.

Uses: Ground cover, bedding, edging, containers, hanging baskets, rock gardens, rock walls.

Color: Blue, white, violet, purple, reddish-purple.

Height: 4 to 8 inches.

How to Start: Best to sow indoors 10 to 12 weeks before final frost, as the growth of seedlings is slow. 70–75°, 14–21 days.

Where to Plant: Best in a fertile, sandy soil high in organic matter. Full sun or partial shade, although the latter is best in areas of hot summers. Does not withstand heat well.

Spacing: 4 to 6 inches.

Care: Keep soil moist. Cut back lightly after first wave of bloom to encourage optimum flowers during the summer. Will cease blooming during high heat, but usually recovers as temperatures cool down.

Native to: South Africa; Cape of Good Hope.

Lobelias provide some of the most intense, vivid blues known to the gardener. These low, dense, trailing plants are smothered with flowers over a long season. They are ideal for edging, and equally charming planted in small patches throughout the rock garden or allowed to trail over a wall. One famous gardener advocated using Lobelia to suggest water in the garden; plant it to cascade down a stony bank like a stream, ending below in a great pool of blue. Occasional tufts of the white form can even create the illusion of foam-flecked waves. Lobelia is great in containers, too, where its soft, fluffy, trailing habit hides the harsh edge of a box or pot. Its uses are limited only by the imagination.

Gardeners in cool climates where lobelia and marigolds can be timed to bloom together can have perhaps the most dramatic of all flower color combinations: a deep gold or golden orange dwarf French marigold edged with a deep purple variety of lobelia; and it must be seen to be believed.

Lobularia maritima
(Sweet Alyssum) H.

Uses: Edging, rock gardens, rock walls, containers, among paving stones.

Color: Mauve, rose, lavender, or white.

Height: 4 to 8 inches.

How to Start: Easy to sow outdoors in place in early spring, or start indoors 4 to 6 weeks prior to the final frost.

Lobularia maritima, rose and white varieties

Lobelia erinus

Do not cover seeds as they require light to germinate. Transplant seedlings only when small. Water young seedlings sparingly and keep warm (70°), as they are prone to damping off. 65–70°, 7–14 days.

Where to Plant: Best in well-drained soil of average fertility, but will perform well in poor soils. Full sun, but tolerates light shade.

Spacing: 4 to 6 inches.

Care: Best when kept moist, although tolerant of drought and heat. Cut back occasionally to improve appearance, compactness, and flowering.

Native to: The Mediterranean region.

Sweet alyssum is a low, trailing annual whose mounds of medium-green foliage are smothered with small erect thimbles of fragrant flowers from late April until frost. Alternate colors are planted in edging and bedding patterns to the point of cliché, but there are many other ways to use alyssum effctively. It is excellent naturalized in rock gardens or between paving stones, where it will reseed from year to year. The fragrant flowers are a delight when planted high enough to be scented, such as at the top or side of a wall or in a hanging basket. Alyssum makes a superb informal ground cover, especially under taller, open, leggy plants such as roses or hollyhocks, and when planted over bulbs will hide messy decaying foliage at the end of the season.

Remember that even at its best alyssum presents an uneven, rolling appearance as a ground cover, and in hot weather can grow ragged and patchy or even cease blooming altogether. Thus it is best in an informal situation, such as in splashes trailing over a garden. Once established, it will persist, reseeding prolifically, so be sure to plant it where this is not a problem. Reseeded alyssum tends to be taller, with washed-out colors. Volunteer seedlings might be best pulled or hoed out. In mild climates it may act as a perennial—particularly in frost-free coastal California, where it blooms the year round.

Matthiola incana

(Stock) Hardy biennial grown as an annual.

Uses: Cut flowers, borders, bedding, containers.

Color: White, ivory, pink, red, lavender, and purple.

Height: 12 to 30 inches.

How to Start: For summer bloom, sow outdoors in place after last frost. For spring bloom, sow indoors 6 to 8 weeks prior. Do not cover seed, as light is required for germination. 70°, 7–10 days. In mild climates seed can be sown outdoors in late fall for late winter and early spring bloom.

Where to Plant: Prefers moist, well-drained soil high in organic matter. Full sun or light shade. Does not flower well in heat, so provide cool location.

Spacing: 10 to 15 inches.

Care: Water adequately but never late in the day. Do not overwater as stocks are prone to root rot. Plant them far enough apart to allow good air circulation. Fertilize monthly.

Native to: The Mediterranean coast.

For the gardener who loves fragrance, stocks are indispensable. In the daytime the scent is subtle and often elusive, prompting many sniffing searches for the mysterious source. But on cool, moist, overcast days, and especially in the twilight hours, the spiced-honey fragrance becomes almost magical.

Stocks grow best in cool, moist weather, and their longest season of bloom will be found in coastal regions of mild, humid summers. In the northern states and Canada, stock can be started indoors early. The plants are grown to good size and starved before being set close together in the spring garden. This can shock them out of vegetative growth and into bloom. In mild western states the early dwarf varieties are a staple for winter bloom, along with pansies and calendulas.

The modern, highly bred forms are quite formal in appearance, with stiffly erect stems tightly covered with double pastel flowers. Probably the best use of stock is for cutting and flower arrangements, where its evening scent and formal shape are most appreciated. But you can also use them in the border, wherever a touch of formality and fragrance is needed.

Matthiola longipetala (Night-Scented Stock) takes the evening fragrance syndrome to the extreme. During the day it is a sad-looking flower, with limp white blossoms hanging onto the rough foliage like bits of wet tissue. But in the cool of the evening, the flowers stretch out into ghostly white crosses and release a powerful perfume that far outshadows that of their highly bred cousins. Tuck it into corners upwind of windows and porches, or along a path that is good for evening walks.

Mimulus × hybridus 'Grandiflorus'

(Monkey Flower) HH.

Uses: Bedding, borders, stream or poolside gardens, rock gardens, rock walls, containers.

Color: Yellows and reds, often in combination.

Height: 6 to 8 inches.

How to Start: Sow indoors 10 to 12 weeks prior to final frost. Do not cover the fine seeds. 70–75°, 7–14 days.

Where to Plant: Prefers moist, well-drained loam rich in organic matter. Partial to moderate shade. Best in a cool, moist location near water, as it is found in nature.

Spacing: 6 inches.

Care: Keep well watered and fertilize regularly. May require grooming of spent blossoms.

Native to: Chile.

As the choices for annuals to grow in the shade is relatively small, it is curious that this colorful plant is not more commonly used. If you're planting with a bed in light to moderate shade and want more than just begonias and impatiens, consider the monkey flower. The plant forms neat, diminutive mounds generously covered with flowers over a long

Matthiola incana

Mimulus × hybridus 'Grandiflorus'

season in summer. The blossoms are gaily colored and up close do resemble a monkey's face. Equally at home in formal beds and borders, or naturalized near water, they will even adjust to a boggy situation or occasional flooding. It is also attractive in pots and containers if kept well watered. Protect this plant from heat and bright sun, and mulch it well where frequent watering is necessary.

Mirabilis jalapa

(Four o'Clock; Beauty of the Night; Marvel of Peru) Perennial usually grown as an annual.

Uses: Beds, borders, low temporary hedge or shrub.
Color: White, yellow, red, pink, often bicolored, and often with 2 or 3 colors appearing on the same plant.
Height: 18 to 36 inches.
How to Start: Can easily sow outdoors after final frost, or indoors 4 to 6 weeks ahead. 70°, 7–10 days.
Where to Plant: Any soil, preferably well-drained. Full sun, but tolerates light shade. Withstands humidity, heat, drought, and air pollution.
Spacing: 18 to 24 inches.
Care: Water plentifully and fertilize monthly. May self-sow freely. Perennial in mild climates. In harsher climates, the heavy roots can be dug after the top dies down from frost, stored in a cool, dry place over winter, and replanted the following spring.
Native to: Tropical Americas, especially Central America and Peru.

The four o'clock, while nondescript during the day, is hard to beat for evening beauty and fragrance. In fact, it is also known as "beauty of the night." Each rounded, shrublike plant is liberally sprinkled with trumpet-shaped blossoms, and has the unusual quality of often bearing flowers of many different colors at once. The blossoms remain tightly closed all day until late afternoon, when they open to exude a rich, heavy fragrance. If lit at night a further drama is revealed, as they are attractive to a wide range of beautiful moths.

Four o'clocks are exceedingly easy to grow. The foliage is clean enough to use as a low hedge or a shrubby foundation planting. Its best use, however, is for early evening and night effect—in masses around the patio or under windows, or in large pots. Naturalize them along a rustic path to spice up romantic nighttime walks. They self-sow readily and are delightful in the wild transition between meadow and woods.

Moluccella laevis

(Bells of Ireland) H.

Uses: Cut flowers, dried flowers, rear of border.
Color: Chartreuse, fading to light beige when dried.
Height: 24 to 36 inches.
How to Start: Easily sown outside in place in early spring as soon as ground can be worked. Sow in late summer for a fall crop. Sow indoors

8 to 10 weeks ahead of final frost. Do not cover the seeds as they require light to germinate. 55°, 25–35 days.
Where to Plant: Average garden loam with good drainage. Full sun to partial shade.
Spacing: 12 inches.
Care: Water regularly and feed monthly for the tallest spikes. Staking is necessary. Will self-sow readily.
Native to: Asia Minor.

The apple-green "bells" of *Moluccella laevis* are beloved by flower arrangers everywhere. They are borne densely packed up and down tall, strong stems, and provide an unusually cool color for the vase. In the rear of the border it combines particularly well with yellows and pinks. In sunny spots protected from wind, it graces any wild garden and reseeds plentifully.

The flower's fresh, light green color seems to last forever in the vase. When hung upside down in a dark, dry, warm place to dry, they turn a beautiful shade of light tan, ideal for delicate winter arrangements, particularly when combined with other soft colors and textures, such as those of dried grasses and seed pods.

As a native of the Near East, the plant appreciates long, mild summers.

Bells of Ireland matures rather quickly, and produces spikes reliably, except in extreme northern areas where summer frosts can nip the tender growth.

Myosotis sylvatica

(Forget-Me-Not) Biennial often treated as annual.

Uses: Ground cover, bedding, naturalizing, edging, borders, water and bog gardens.
Color: Usually, blue, also pink and white.
Height: 6 to 12 inches.
How to Start: Sow outdoors in late summer for spring bloom, in spring or early summer for fall bloom. Or sow indoors 4 to 6 weeks before planting out in early spring. 55–65°, 7–14 days.
Where to Plant: Fertile, moist, well-drained soil rich in organic matter. Performs well in wet soil. Prefers partial shade, but tolerates full sun. Best in regions of long, cool springs. Elsewhere, spring crops will set seeds and die out. Then, after late-summer rains, a second crop will come up and give you fall color.
Spacing: 8 to 12 inches.
Care: Water and feed liberally. Easy.
Native to: Temperate Europe.

In late summer or early fall, after planting a bed of bulbs, cast about a generous supply of forget-me-not seeds. You will be rewarded in spring with a beautiful blue haze as a perfect backdrop for daffodils and tulips, one that will keep the bed colorful well into early summer. Forget-me-not reseeds abundantly, to perform year after year. Its tiny blue, pink, or white flowers bloom generously on delicate, multi-branched stems.

Myosotis are native to the moist, rich woodlands of Europe, where they bloom

Moluccella laevis

lis jalapa 'Jingles Mixed'

Myosotis sylvatica

early in spring just as leaves emerge from the trees. They will thrive happily when naturalized in moist meadows, under light shade, and especially in the cool, rich soil of streambanks and watersides. Their delicacy seems to beg naturalizing in generous drifts.

Nemesia strumosa
(Pouch Nemesia) HH.

Uses: Edging, bedding, borders, rock gardens and walls, containers, cut flowers.
Color: White, yellow, orange, pink, red, mauve.
Height: 12 to 18 inches.
How to Start: Sow outdoors in place after final frost, but best to sow indoors 4 to 6 weeks ahead. 55–70°, 7–14 days.
Where to Plant: Fertile, moist, well-drained soil high in organic matter. Will not tolerate excessive heat or humidity, so should be grown in climates where the summers are cool and dry. Full sun or partial shade.
Spacing: 6 inches.
Care: Water and fertilize liberally. Pinch young plants to encourage dense growth.
Native to: South Africa.

A bed of Nemesia is like a carnival in bloom, for nearly every gay color of the rainbow is found in this plant. Its curiously shaped flowers have a thick, bulbous lower lip, similar to snapdragon and linaria, to which they are related. All three, in fact, are delightful planted together, repeating form and color but in different sizes. Nemesias make brilliant masses of color in beds all to

themselves, as an edging, in front of the border, or set about the patio in boxes and pots. Their diminutive size and preference for sharp drainage make them a natural for the rock garden.

Unfortunately, Nemesias will not withstand the intense summer heat of the central and southern states. To get any color at all in these areas, and that only for a short season, it is necessary to set out well-started plants in spring. They were among the first annuals to be imported from South Africa, where they grow on the coastal fringes that enjoy mild, long, dry summers. In areas with cool summers, however, they can provide spectacular color from spring until frost.

Be sure to pinch young plants to get the densest growth and the most flowers, and cut the plants back halfway after the first wave of bloom.

Nemophila menziesii
(Baby Blue Eyes) HH.

Uses: Edging, beds, rock gardens and walls, ground cover, containers.
Color: Blue.
Height: 6 to 12 inches.
How to Start: Best to sow outdoors in early spring as soon as soil can be worked. Can sow indoors 4 to 6 weeks prior to planting out in mid-spring. Constant 55°, 7–12 days.
Where to Plant: Light, sandy loam; sharp drainage a must. Full sun to partial shade.

Spacing: 6 to 9 inches.
Care: Water moderately, fertilize only lightly if at all. Self-sows freely.
Native to: California.

That the baby blue eyes is not a more popularly grown plant is cause for wonder. Neat, bright green mounds of tufted foliage; fragrant, pale blue, cup-shaped flowers with a cheerful white center; undemanding culture for sun or shade—all these facts point to a most desirable plant.

The baby blue eyes is a woodland plant long thought to require shading from hot sun; but recent experience has proven this untrue: it performs equally well in full sun if generously watered. Use it as a ground cover for color from June to frost. Plant it in great beds all to itself, or among other low-growing annuals. Mix it with other blues, whites, and pinks at the front of the border, or use it to edge walks and patios. It is especially charming peeking out from behind large stones in the rock garden or casually tucked into the pockets among paving stones. The uses are infinite for this plant. Perhaps the public has yet to discover it.

Nicotiana alata
(Flowering Tobacco; Nicotiana) T.

Uses: Bedding, containers, cut flowers.
Color: White, mauve, red, maroon, pink, yellow, green, yellow-green.
Height: 12 to 36 inches.
How to Start: Can easily sow

outdoors in place after final frost. Or sow indoors 6 to 8 weeks ahead. Do not cover seeds as they require light to germinate. Constant 70°, 10–20 days.
Where to Plant: Best in fertile, well-drained, moist soil high in organic matter. Partial shade best, but it will tolerate full sun where humid; flowers will fade some in full sun in dry climates.
Spacing: 8 to 12 inches, more with the old-fashioned types.
Care: Fertilize regularly; keep soil moist. Will self-sow freely.
Native to: Brazil.

Nicotiana reaches the height of grace when massed in large beds. Each plant is anchored by a low rosette of large leaves from which spring tall, slender stems. Long, thin tubes at right angles to the stem open into star-shaped color. The nodding, delicate effect is enhanced by planting in great masses, especially when in a gentle wind.

Often touted as powerfully fragrant, the day-blooming hybrids available today are sorely disappointing. Occasionally a fresh, sweet scent can be detected in the vicinity of a bed, especially on cool evenings; but the famous perfume, sadly, has been lost. It can be found only in the tall, old-fashioned, evening-blooming kinds.

Consider Nicotiana when looking for a tall, delicate statement in the mixed border. It is surprisingly effective planted in clumps in large pots. Try not

Nemesia strumosa

Nemophila menziesii

Nicotiana alata 'Nicki Rose'

to grow Nicotiana near where you intend to grow tomatoes. Nicotiana attracts many pests and diseases that may then attack the tomatoes, such as tobacco mosaic virus. While the hardy Nicotiana will be little troubled, your tomatoes may not survive.

Nicotiana is gaining favor as an alternative to petunias in areas where the humidity related disease botrytis can snip the blossoms off for several weeks in late summer.

Nierembergia hippomanica
(Cup Flower) Tender perennial grown as an annual.

Uses: Edging, bedding, containers, rock gardens, rock walls.
Color: Blue-violet, purple.
Height: 6 to 12 inches.
How to Start: Sow indoors 10 to 12 weeks prior to setting out after the final frost. It will not grow rapidly until the soil has warmed. 70–75°, 14–21 days.
Where to Plant: Fertile, sandy, moist, well-drained soil high in organic matter. Full sun to partial shade. The latter is preferred in areas with hot summers.
Spacing: 6 to 12 inches.
Care: Easy. Keep moist, do not overwater.
Native to: Argentina.

While little known and usually hard to find as plants, the cup flower is a diminutive delight in the garden. Neat, spreading mounds of fine-textured foliage are smothered with blue-violet flowers all summer long. Flowers hold their color without fading in the brightest sun.

Nierembergia is outstanding in large beds or as a ground cover, but even more elegant and appropriate grown in small patches in the rock garden. It also behaves well as an edging to a border or walkway, and you can plant it in pots, hanging baskets, and window boxes. It is also a logical substitute for trailing lobelia where the latter dies out due to heat.

For its easy, long-season blue-violet color and restrained size, the cup flower deserves greater popularity.

Nigella damascena
(Love-in-a-Mist) H.

Uses: Border, cut flowers, dried seed pods for arranging.
Color: Blue, white, pink.
Height: 12 to 30 inches.
How to Start: Difficult to transplant, Nigella is best sown outdoors in early spring as soon as ground can be worked. Or sow indoors in individual peat pots 4 to 6 weeks ahead. 65–70°, 10–15 days.
Where to Plant: Sandy loam or gravelly soil. Must have sharp drainage. Full sun.
Spacing: 8 to 15 inches.
Care: Fertilize monthly; water only when soil is dry. May require staking. As flowering season is short, make successive plantings from early spring to early summer for continuous summer bloom.
Native to: Mediterranean region.

The open, feathery habit and soft colors of Nigella are a tremendous asset when mixed into the informal border or cottage garden. Alone or in formal situations it is a little too sprawly to be welcome. The romantic common name is due to the many threadlike, feathery bracts which surround the flowers in a cloud of green. Love-in-a-mist is an excellent choice for cutting as the flowers last well and bring an unusual effect to any arrangement. The seed pods are even more desirable for the same purpose, when cut after they have ripened and dried.

As the plant reseeds generously, it will probably remain in your garden for years to come. It is especially charming naturalized in a grassy meadow. In the Mediterranean climates of southern Europe it has escaped to roam the hills in clouds of blue. While the season of bloom is not long, this can easily be rectified by dropping some seed every two or three weeks throughout the spring and early summer.

Papaver rhoeas
(Field Poppy) H.
Papaver nudicaule
(Iceland Poppy)
Perennial often treated as an annual or biennial.

Uses: Border, rock gardens, cut flowers.
Color: Red, purple, white, pink, salmon, orange. Early summer season.
Height: Papaver rhoeas, 1 to 2 feet; P. nudicaule, 2 to 3 feet, less where spring is short.
How to Start: For summer flowers sow outdoors in place in early spring as soon as ground can be worked. Most poppies resent transplanting, but you can try starting them indoors 6 to 8 weeks prior to the final frost, in individual peat pots. 55°, 10–15 days. *P. nudicaule* can be sown outdoors in late summer for earlier bloom the next year.
Where to Plant: Sharply drained, fertile, sandy soil rich in organic matter. Full sun. Best performance and longest bloom season in regions of cool summers.
Spacing: 9 to 12 inches.
Care: Water only moderately and fertilize monthly. *P. rhoeas* should be planted successively throughout spring to ensure longer summer bloom.
Native to: Papaver rhoeas, Europe; P. nudicaule, the Arctic and circumpolar regions of North America and Eurasia.

Vast regions of Europe and Asia are blessed with the wild exuberance of the field poppy. Tiny silken hairs on buds and long stems glisten in the sunlight. Brilliantly colored petals like crinkled silk surround a dark eye. The value of each flower is intensified by its short life, especially in wind and rain, and the plant sends up blooms only for 2 to 3 weeks before dying to the ground. But this apparent fragility is met by abundant fertility. One authority, with characteristic medieval patience, counted over thirty-two thousand seeds in a single capsule.

The field poppy's short life makes it unsuitable for planting in solid beds. But is excellent for mixing in the border, where

Nigella damascena 'Persian Jewels'

Nierembergia hippomanica

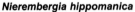

Papaver nudicaule

Papaver nudicaule

other plants soon fill vacant spots, or for naturalizing in a meadow. And it is possible with successive plantings to have flowers from late May through July. Sow them outdoors in place, as these plants are difficult to transplant. The seeds are exceptionally tiny, so mix them with twice their amount of fine sand and sow very thinly. Field poppies are choice cut flowers, although short-lived as such. To make them last longest, cut in the early morning as the buds first show color, sear the cut ends with a flame, and place them in hot (not boiling) water for a moment or two.

Many varieties of field poppies have been bred over the years. The most commonly available (and perhaps the best) are the Shirley poppies. These have large single blossoms in the widest range of clear colors, with white or yellow centers.

The Iceland poppy (*Papaver nudicaule*) is a true biennial that should be sown outdoors in summer or early fall for early summer bloom. It is most popular in the warm West and Deep South, where late-summer plantings will produce winter bloom over a long period.

Less well known is its excellence for gardens across the cool northland, where it will bloom with bearded iris. Here, seeds are started early indoors, 2 or 3 to a 4-inch pot, and the plants, after hardening off, are carefully set in the garden as a clump.

Iceland poppy produces an abundance of large, silky flowers atop long stems. They

make excellent cut flowers when treated as described above; and cutting also prolongs bloom.

Pelargonium × hortorum
(Geranium) Tender perennial grown as an annual.

Uses: Bedding, borders, house plant, containers, hanging baskets.

Color: Red, pink, salmon, orange, white. Foliage of fancy-leaf varieties appears in variegations of up to 4 colors, including red, salmon, yellow, pink, bronze, maroon, green, and white.

Height: 12 to 24 inches.

How to Start: All can easily be propagated from stem cuttings (the usual method for fancy-leaf varieties). For many years these hybrids were propagated only by cuttings due to the extreme variations that resulted from seed. Now hybrids such as the 'Carefree' strain have been developed and are guaranteed to breed true from seed. Seeds may be sown outdoors in place in mild climates. In the North, seeds should be started 12 to 16 weeks before setting out after the last frost. Seedlings need strong light to produce short, stocky plants. When they reach thumbnail size, carefully pry out for transplanting in 3-inch pots. 68–70°, 5–15 days.

Where to Plant: Prefers rich, moist, well-drained soil high in organic matter. Seems to like slightly acid soil. Full sun. Newer cultivars tolerate heat but can be knocked out by prolonged high heat and humidity.

Spacing: 8 to 15 inches.

Care: Water and feed liberally. Remove flower heads as they fade.

Native to: Of hybrid origin. Parents native to South Africa.

Rare is the gardener who at some time has not grown a pelargonium. Easy and vigorous, it is one of the most highly bred and readily available of all annuals. Flowers are intensely colored and produced freely over a long season from May to frost.

In the mildest parts of California and Florida, pelargoniums are grown as perennials for year-round bloom, sometimes trained to climb up fences or arbors, or planted to spill down steep banks. In harsher climates, year-round color is still possible if you bring the plants indoors for the winter; in fact, pelargoniums are almost as popular for house plants as for beds and borders.

If you do choose to grow them in pots, be a little skimpy with space for the roots. Pelargoniums flower better with slight root constriction, so use 5- to 7-inch pots for individual plants, or crowd several into larger containers.

Groom geraniums regularly for appearance and to encourage more blooms; the long flower stalks snap off easily. If the plant becomes a bit tall and leggy, don't be afraid to cut it back; and if you like, save the cuttings to start new plants.

Some of the newer hybrids are especially exciting for their

Petunia × hybrida, mixed cultivars

Pelargonium × hortorum 'Salmon Flash'

improved heat tolerance, non-fading flowers, and resistance to disease. These should be preferred over the older types.

Petunia × hybrida
(Petunia) HH.

Uses: Bedding, borders, containers, hanging baskets.
Color: Violet, pink, salmon, red, purple, yellow, white, in all shades; solid and bicolored.
Height: 10 to 18 inches.
How to Start: Sow indoors 10 to 12 weeks prior to final frost. Do not cover the fine seeds, as light is required for germination, but use a glass or similar smooth object to press them into the soil. Usually purchased as young plants from the nursery. 70–80°, 5–15 days.
Where to Plant: Sharply drained, light sandy soil is best. Full sun. Shade discourages flowering. The single types will tolerate heavier, more alkaline soils.
Spacing: 12 inches.
Care: Water moderately and feed liberally, at least once a month. In containers allow to dry out between waterings. Pinch or shear plants twice: once when 6 inches tall, and again after the first wave of flowers. This will promote density and greater flowering.
Native to: Argentina.

If one plant were to encapsulate the phrase, "gardening with annuals," it would be the petunia. Dependability, versatility, and variety are its hallmarks, making it little wonder that this long-season flower is the most popular annual in America. Vigorous breeding efforts have created an astounding array of flower size, form, and color from which to choose. Broad, funnel-shape blossoms can be found as double as a carnation or smoothly single. Petal edges can be frilled, fluffed, fluted, or straight and simple. Some flowers are as large as 7 inches across, others a bare 2 inches. And the hues range among every shade. (Beware of plants advertised as "blue," as they are more likely lavender or violet-purple. And the so-called "yellow" varieties are actually a cream or a very pale yellow, although a breakthrough with a good yellow is expected any time now.)

While petunia varieties are far too many to list, they generally can be divided into two major types, the grandifloras and the multifloras. The grandifloras produce the largest blossoms, and can be broken into single and double categories of bloom. The multifloras have smaller flowers, also divided into singles and doubles, but they are produced in greater quantity. The single-flowered types are excellent for beds and borders. The double-flowered types, as they tend to fall over in the garden, are best reserved for containers. The multiflora petunias deserve to be planted more widely because they are resistant to botrytis, which can strip blossoms of all plants during humid weather.

Grandifloras and the frilly, double varieties of multifloras both look quite ragged after a summer storm beats on their delicate petals. But after a day or two, new flowers emerge and the plants recover.

Cascade types are also popular and can be found in all the above categories. Their longer stems make them ideal for hanging baskets or trailing over a wall.

Many gardeners prefer buying F₁ hybrids. They are the most vigorous and floriferous, but are hand pollinated, making them also the most expensive. Petunias, like their closely related cousin, *Nicotiana,* attract an abundance of beautiful moths at night. They are especially pleasing planted near the patio or under a window, wherever you can enjoy the evening show.

Petunias are easy to start outside after the last frost, but develop slowly in cool spring weather. Start them indoors for earlier bloom, or purchase young plants in flats from the nursery. Petunias are one of the few annuals whose young seedlings can withstand a full, hot sun. As with snapdragons, pinching is an absolute necessity for dense, full-flowering plants; it will, however, delay flowering by 7 to 10 days.

Phlox drummondii
(Annual Phlox) HH.

Uses: Bedding, edging, containers, rock and wall gardens, cut flowers, naturalizing.
Color: White, pink, red, salmon, and mauve, often in bicolor combinations.
Height: 6 to 20 inches.
How to Start: As phlox resents transplanting, it should be sown outdoors in place in early spring as soon as soil can be worked. If grown in containers, sow directly indoors 4 to 6 weeks before setting outside. When thinning, remember that the weakest seedlings often develop the strongest color. 55–65°, 10–15 days.
Where to Plant: Must have well-drained soil, preferably moist, sandy, and high in organic matter. Full sun. Tolerates heat, although flowers will decline in the hottest part of the summer.
Spacing: 6 inches, but not critical. Phlox will tolerate moderate crowding. Much of the flower's charm is in the enormous range of colors and bicolors. Excessive thinning decreases the color range. You can plant 3 or 4 seeds per 4- or 5-inch pot and transplant as a clump.
Care: Easy. Feed liberally and keep moist. Avoid watering late in the day. Remove blossoms as they fade.
Native to: Texas.

The name *Phlox* originates from a Greek word meaning flame, and this is certainly appropriate to its brilliant, fiery colors. *Phlox drummondii,* sometimes called Texas pride, is native to the sandy soils of that state, but even though it requires a well-drained soil, it also fares best with abundant moisture. Take care, though; most of the pests that cause phlox trouble, notably powdery mildew and crown rot, are caused by moisture hanging onto foliage or at the base

Petunia × hybrida 'Red Bouquet'

Phlox drummondii 'Grandiflora Finest Mixed'

of the plant in the cool of the evening. So water early in the day.

Annual phlox is available in a wide range of colors and forms. The most popular are the dwarf types, but the larger varieties (to 20 inches) can provide interesting contrast in height. Most bear rounded flowers bunched together in tight heads. A few varieties have lacy, star-shaped blossoms in looser clusters.

While the plants survive heat quite well, flowers often will suffer. In hot-summer areas you can expect a ragged decline in July and August, but their appearance will pick up again as the weather cools.

Portulaca grandiflora
(Rose Moss) T.

Uses: Bedding, edging, ground cover, rock gardens, walls, containers, dry banks, cracks in paving.

Color: Red, yellow, white, pink, salmon, and purple.

Height: 4 to 8 inches.

How to Start: Easy to sow directly outside after final frost, or indoors 4 to 6 weeks ahead. 70–80°, 10–15 days.

Where to Plant: Hot, dry, perfectly drained sandy soil. Full sun. Withstands heat and drought well.

Spacing: 12 to 24 inches.

Care: Water infrequently. Avoid overwatering.

Native to: Brazil.

Portulaca will thrive in situations that most annuals avoid like the plague. Intense heat, dry rocky soil, even nearly pure sand are all conditions

that it loves. The plant forms loose, trailing mats of brittle stems and tiny, fleshy leaves covered with brilliantly colored flowers. The petals have a distinctive sheen, like watered silk. Many varieties have double or ruffled flowers. Nearly all are available only in mixtures. A few specialty seed houses offer straight colors. Unfortunately, the flowers close late in the day and during cloudy weather, which diminishes their use in climates of frequent haze or clouds. But this problem is being worked on by several large breeders, and we can expect a breakthrough soon.

Portulaca makes an excellent ground cover for sunny, dry banks and areas of poor soil. And it reaches its height of beauty scattered in small patches throughout the rock garden or between paving stones. Plant it in high pockets and cracks in walls, pack it tightly into containers, or plant it in rose beds to act as an understory for taller plants. Portulaca reseeds plentifully so once you plant it, expect it to be around for a while.

Reseda odorata
(Mignonette) H.

Uses: Cut flowers, fragrance, containers, border, bedding.

Color: Greenish yellow to yellowish white.

Height: 12 to 18 inches.

How to Start: Best to sow outside in early spring as soon as soil can be worked, as it

resents transplanting. Do not cover seeds, as light is required for germination.

Where to Plant: Fertile, well-drained, moist soil high in organic matter. Full sun to partial shade. Best in regions of cool summers.

Spacing: 10 to 12 inches.

Care: Keep moist. Feed lightly once a month.

Native to: North Africa.

Mignonette is a modest little plant. At first sight you wonder why anyone should want to grow these homely, sprawling greenish-yellow flowers. But take a deep breath on a cool summer evening and prepare to be overwhelmed by one of the most intoxicating fragrances known to the annual gardener. Mix it craftily into the border, where its unobtrusive appearance will spark intense searches for the source of the scent. Plant it under windows, near doorways, walks, porches, and patios where its delicious scent will be most appreciated. Mignonette performs beautifully in pots (at least 6 inches in diameter), and containers give you the advantage of being able to follow changing breezes, to place it so the wind will carry the fragrance where you like.

While several more brightly colored varieties have recently been bred, none match the superb fragrance of the plain old-fashioned plant, which the English poet Cowper once called "the fragrant weed."

In hot-summer regions its bloom season is greatly reduced. Try to place it in the coolest spot in your garden.

Ricinus communis
(Castor Bean) T.

Uses: Background, screen, ornamental seed pod, temporary shrub. Caution: seeds are deadly poisonous. Two can kill a child.

Color: Grown for large size and huge, tropical, coarse foliage, which is mostly deep green, but in some types bronze or reddish, in others deep red- or white-variegated. Some have bright red or purple stems.

Height: 5 to 10 feet.

How to Start: Sow outdoors after final frost, or start indoors 6 to 8 weeks ahead. Soak the seed in lukewarm water for 24 hours or file the seedcoat. Minimize handling of the seeds; some people are allergic to them. 70–75°, 15–20 days.

Where to Plant: Prefers rich, well-drained soil high in organic matter. Full sun. Likes heat and abundant moisture.

Spacing: 4 to 5 feet.

Care: Fertilize and water heavily. Staking may be required in windy locations.

Native to: Tropical Africa.

No other annual—indeed, few other ornamental plants of any kind—can compete with the castor bean for its lush, tropical leaves, often 3 feet wide. Unfortunately this plant is marred with a serious defect, as its seeds contain a virulent poison that means certain severe illness, and quite possibly death, to any person who eats them. The castor bean should *never* be planted where children might play.

Ricinus communis with blue and red Salvia and Ageratum in foreground

Portulaca grandiflora

Reseda odorata 'Sweet Scented'

If you can find a safe spot, however, then use it wherever you want to suggest the deep, dark jungles of its African homeland. Combine it with other bold-textured foliage plants such as *Amaranthus*; set off its coarse texture by adding the soft, swaying plumes of grasses; highlight its deep colors with the silver dusty miller. The castor bean makes an excellent background for the border, and is a superb statement standing alone, like a small tree or large shrub. Many varieties are available.

If you can't find castor bean seeds locally, there may be an ordinance against its sale. In addition, where frosts are light, castor beans can escape and become a nuisance weed. In warmer climates it will act as a perennial.

Rudbeckia hirta var. pulcherrima 'Gloriosa Daisy'

(Gloriosa Daisy, Brown-Eyed Susan) Perennial often treated as an annual.

Uses: Borders, bedding, background, cut flowers.
Color: Golden yellow, bronze, orange, or mahogany, often bicolored.
Height: 2 to 3 feet.
How to Start: For flowers the first year from seed, start indoors 6 to 8 weeks before final frost. Where summers are long, sow in spring in place. 70–75°, 5–10 days.
Where to Plant: Best in rich, moist, well-drained soil high in organic matter. Tolerates poor, dry soil. Appreciates hot summers.

Spacing: 12 to 24 inches.
Care: Keep soil moderately moist for best performance. Taller varieties may need some staking. Regular fungicide program will help prevent mildew. Reseeds freely each year.
Native to: Midwestern and eastern United States.

Many treasured garden flowers call the prairie their home, but rudbeckia is probably the most visible.

There are many species of rudbeckia, and most are perennial. All are robust and vigorous. Gloriosa daisies are actually short-lived perennials, treated as annuals, that bloom well the first year from seed, if planted early enough. They will survive any poor soil, if well-drained, and flower wonderfully in the most intense summer heat. These are rugged flowers with foliage to match, and look best in rows or groups behind shorter flowers that can hide their rough leaves. Many varieties are available, with single or double flowers in solid and bicolored yellow, gold, orange, and bronze, all with chocolate brown centers. Regally handsome in the rear of the border, they also make stunning beds all to themselves. The flowers are long-lasting when cut and excellent for arranging. Both wild and in the garden rudbeckias have an assertive, hot quality that seems to need the company of soft, cool ornamental grasses. Arrange them together in borders and in vases.

Salpiglossis sinuata

(Painted Tongue) HH.

Uses: Rear of the border, cut flowers.
Color: Purple, red, yellow, bronze, blue, pink in various combinations.
Height: 2 to 3 feet.
How to Start: Best to start indoors in individual peat pots 8 weeks prior to the final frost, although can be sown outdoors. The fine seeds should not be covered with soil, but they require darkness to germinate. Place flats in a dark room or cover with opaque material. 70–75°, 15–20 days.
Where to Plant: Must have excellent, sharp drainage. Best in rich, moist, light, sandy loam high in organic matter and on the alkaline side. Full sun. Performs best in regions with cool summers.
Spacing: 8 to 12 inches.
Care: Water moderately, fertilize lightly. Plants may require support. Protect from wind.
Native to: Chile.

Here is a "brag flower." In horticultural circles, if you can do a good job of growing salpiglossis you have *arrived*. The painted tongue is a close relation to Petunia and Nicotania, but unlike its cousins it is a little tricky to grow. The effort is worthwhile, however, as the flowers are trumpet-shaped, often bicolored, and richly veined. The plants fit best into the middle or rear of the mixed border, where their elongated stems blend gracefully with other plants.

Salpiglossis dislikes wet, soggy conditions as much as dry ones, so water carefully. Do not overfertilize, as it is

sensitive to nitrogen. Instead, give it infrequent, light applications of a slow-release fertilizer. It is native to coastal and high-altitude Chile, where the summers are mild and cool, and will not perform well in regions of intense heat or aridity.

The "secret" to growing good salpiglossis is to start seeds early enough indoors to have good-size plants ready to set out as soon as frost danger is past. It blooms from July till frost.

Salvia splendens

(Scarlet Sage) T.

Salvia farinacea

(Blue Sage) HH.

Uses: Bedding, border, containers, cut flowers.
Color: Salvia splendens, bright red, pink, mauve, purple, white; *S. farinacea,* violet blue, silvery blue.
Height: Salvia splendens, 6 to 36 inches; *S. farinacea,* 18 to 36 inches.
How to Start: S. splendens should be started 6 to 8 weeks prior to the final frost, while *S. farinacea* should be started 12 weeks ahead. Do not cover the seeds of *S. splendens,* as they require light to germinate. After germination keep night temperatures at 55°. Damping off can be a problem. Be sure to use fresh seed. 70–75°, 12–15 days.
Where to Plant: Well-drained, moist, rich soil high in organic matter. Full sun. Scarlet sage will tolerate partial shade. Partial shade is best for varieties with pastel or cream colors, which fade in full sun.

Rudbeckia hirta var. pulcherrima 'Gloriosa Pinwheel'

Salpiglossis sinuata

Salvia splendens 'Red Pillar'

Spacing: 6 to 12 inches.

Care: Keep well watered, although sage is tolerant of mild drought. Fertilize monthly.

Native to: Salvia splendens, Brazil; *S. farinacea,* New Mexico and Texas.

It's no wonder that the scarlet sage is one of the most popular spike-flowered annuals for large-scale bedding and bright color, especially in parks and other public places.

It requires little attention and provides some of the brightest, most intense reds and scarlets known to the annual gardener. And yet, in spite of its popularity, its versatility has been largely unexploited. *Salvia* is excellent to provide splashes of accent among other annuals in an informal border. Unknown to many, it performs beautifully in light shade, although flowering a bit later. Another delightful attribute unknown to many is that hummingbirds love them. If for no other reason, this makes *Salvia splendens* a delight for pots and patios.

The blue salvia, although lesser known, is an equally useful plant. As its more subtle colors are apt to get lost mixed in the border, its most stunning effect is achieved by massing it in great background sheets. The foliage is nicely grayish, which complements the flower color. In warmer climates it will act as a perennial from year to year.

Both of these sages hold up brilliantly in intense heat, and are long-lasting when cut for the vase.

Sanvitalia procumbens
(Creeping Zinnia) T.

Uses: Edging, bedding, ground cover, rock gardens, walls, hanging baskets, stony banks, cracks in pavement.

Color: Golden yellow with purple centers.

Height: 6 inches.

How to Start: Best to sow in place outside after all danger of frost is past, as it does not transplant well. Do not cover the seeds, as light is required for germination.

Where to Plant: Prefers light, well-drained, sandy soil. Appreciates heat, tolerates drought. Full sun.

Spacing: 4 to 6 inches.

Care: Easy. Do not overwater. Fertilizing not necessary.

Native to: Mexico.

Cheerful golden yellow flowers, like miniature zinnias, are liberally sprinkled on this trailing creeper from June to frost. Native to the hot, dry plains of Mexico, it has an understandable preference for full sun and sandy, well-drained soil, but creeping zinnia is easy to grow nearly anywhere, even tolerating partial shade and alkaline clays without complaint. Use it as a ground cover in hot, dry, difficult spots, such as a rocky, steep bank. Planted in large beds all to itself, it forms a tight, low mass of foliage and flowers that inhibits weeds. As an edging, it is always neat and crisp in the front of the border or along a path. In rock gardens it will creep about in the most charming way, forming irregular spreading mats or dripping loose gold down the side of a wall.

Be sure not to pamper this plant, as too much water and fertilizer will damage rather than help. The phrase "benign neglect" seemingly was created for *Sanvitalia procumbens.* For the busy gardener, they are good words to hear.

Scabiosa atropurpurea
(Pincushion Flower) HH.

Uses: Cut flowers, possibly bedding and borders.

Color: Blue, purple, red, pink, white.

Height: 12 to 36 inches.

How to Start: Sow in place outside after all danger of frost has past. Or sow indoors 4 to 5 weeks ahead. 70–75°, l0–l5 days.

Where to Plant: Rich, well-drained, alkaline soil high in organic matter. Full sun.

Spacing: 8 to l5 inches.

Care: Easy. Water moderately.

Native to: Southern Europe.

It is unfortunate that such a pretty, hardworking flower should be cursed with the distasteful name, *Scabiosa.* Perhaps this is the reason why it is little planted today. The flowers are unusual, fluffy and round with many double petals bristling with hundreds of white or yellow stamens, like pins in a cushion. The earlier varieties possessed a rich, honey fragrance, but the new varieties must be held close to the nose to enjoy the scent. The flowers are held aloft on tall, strong, leafy stems ideal for cutting. The dwarf varieties serve well as bedding, but the taller vari-

eties are best reserved for the cutting garden, where the appearance of the necessary stakes doesn't matter.

The pincushion flower is sensitive to soggy conditions and moisture standing on the foliage for any length of time, so water moderately and always early in the day.

Schizanthus × wisetonensis
(Butterfly Flower; Poor Man's Orchid) HH.

Uses: Bedding, border, containers, cut flowers.

Color: Pastel pinks, yellows, and violets; deep golds, reds, and magenta; combinations.

Height: 12 to 24 inches.

How to Start: Sow indoors 12 weeks prior to last frost. The fine seed should not be covered, but it responds to darkness. Place the flat in a dark room or cover with black plastic. 60–70°, 20–30 days.

Where to Plant: Prefers rich, moist soil high in organic matter. Must have perfect drainage. Will perform best in regions with cool summers. Full sun to light shade, the latter in warm climates.

Spacing: 12 inches.

Care: Water moderately. Easy.

Native to: Chile.

The blooms of schizanthus truly resemble small butterflies, which hover in great masses over delicate, lacy foliage. It is a late bloomer, not reaching its greatest effect until August. As it is native to the Andes Mountains of Chile, it is unfor-

Scabiosa atropurpurea

Schizanthus × wisetonensis

Sanvitalia procumbens

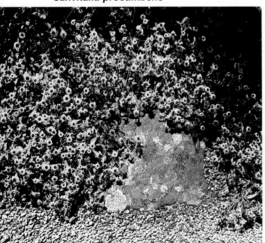

tunately not well adapted to the intense heat so typical of late summers in most places. Its use is severely limited to cool-summer regions in the north, the mountains, and along the coast.

Where it can be grown, the butterfly flower is a perfect choice to succeed beds of early summer and midsummer annuals. It combines well with most colors in the mixed border and is a long-lasting cut flower for arrangements. It is superb in containers, as the blossoms are most freely produced when the roots are a little constricted. Don't try to grow it indoors, however, unless you can give it high humidity and cool, 50° nights. If you are blessed with a greenhouse, then by all means enjoy its color all winter.

Senecio cineraria
(Dusty Miller) Perennial almost always treated as an annual.

Uses: Edging, containers, beds.
Color: Flowers are daisylike and yellow; foliage is silver white.
Height: 8 to l6 inches.
How to Start: Start indoors 8 to 10 weeks prior to the last frost. Do not cover the seed. Sow thinly, and avoid overwatering. Quite susceptible to damping off. Constant 75°, 10–15 days.
Where to Plant: Prefers light, well-drained soil high in organic matter, but performs admirably in dry sandy soils. Tolerates drought. Full sun; tolerates light shade.

Spacing: 8 to 10 inches.
Care: Water lightly. Do not overwater. For optimum foliage effect, remove any flowers as they appear and occasionally shear to prevent legginess.
Native to: The Mediterranean region.

An advantage of using a durable annual with attractive foliage is that you're free from dependence upon the ephemeral, usually delicate, nature of flowers. You can generally rely on the healthy presence of leaves for an entire growing season, from beginning to end.

While the daisylike blossoms of dusty miller are pleasant, the foliage is distinctly the better part of this plant. White, wooly, and finely divided like heavy lace, the leaves are whorled in tight, compact clumps. The plant is perfect for a crisp, neat edging that contrasts nicely with the border or a brick wall. Mix it in large beds for contrast with richer colors, or grow it in pots for the patio. Dusty miller is particularly exciting in a moonlit garden, where its silvery hairs reflect the dimmest light. For this reason it is excellent around outdoor living areas to highlight the edges and structure of your garden.

Dusty miller will need help to keep its dense, compact shape. Remove any flower buds as they start to appear, and occasionally shear back the most rebellious, open plants. Several newer cultivars are tighter and smaller than ever.

In mild, dry climates like its Mediterranean homeland, dusty miller is apt to become a shrubby perennial.

Tagetes erecta
(African Marigold) HH.
Tagetes patula
(French Marigold) HH.
Tagetes erecta × T. patula
(Triploid or 3-N Marigolds) T.

Uses: Bedding, edging, cut flowers, border.
Color: Yellow, orange, bronze.
Height: Tagetes erecta, 6, 10 to 36 inches; *T. patula*, 6 to 18 inches; triploids, 12 to 20 inches.
How to Start: Tagetes patula is easy to sow in place outside after last frost. *T. erecta* takes a long time to reach bloom, and is best started indoors, except where summers are long. All three can be sown indoors 4 to 6 weeks prior to the final frost. 65–75°, 5–7 days.
Where to Plant: Prefers moist, well-drained loam, but tolerates dry soils. High summer heat can cause marigolds to "stall" (temporarily decline, causing growth and bloom), although some triploids are notably resistant.
Spacing: 6 to 18 inches.
Care: Except for triploids, which do not need it, pinch off faded blossoms to encourage denser growth and more flowers.
Native to: Mexico.

Brilliant, easy color is the hallmark of the marigold, and the immense popularity of this cheerful plant has led to extensive hybridizing, resulting in

an array of forms that can be confusing. All bear either single or double flowers in the familiar yellows, golds, and oranges, some bicolored with red or brown stripes.

The African marigold, *Tagetes erecta*, is the tallest type, and is divided into three categories: tall (2 to 3 feet), medium (1 to 2 feet), and dwarf (10 to 12 inches). The African marigold has a rather vertical form that is best massed in groups or beds. The flowers are double and resemble golden or yellow carnations. The taller types will require staking to protect them from bad weather.

The French marigold, *Tagetes patula*, is a bushier plant with finely dissected leaves and smaller single or double flowers, often bicolored, the petals tipped or striped with red or mahogany. Since this plant is more compact and its foliage is often dense clear to the ground, it makes a superb edging as well as colorful beds. And it looks surprisingly natural planted for a random effect about the deliberately "wild" garden.

The triploids resemble large-flowered French marigolds. They are sterile and do not form seeds; thus, they will continue to flower in late summer when other kinds stall or "blank."

Signet marigolds have very small yellow or orange blossoms on spreading mounds of fernlike foliage. They deserve greater popularity, especially for naturalistic effects.

Tagetes erecta 'Climax'

Tagetes patula 'Tina'

Senecio cineraria 'Silver Dust' with tuberous begonias

The ease of achieving healthy, productive marigolds accounts for much of their popularity. While appreciative of rich soil, they produce too much foliage at the expense of flowers if overfertilized. Deadheading helps improve appearance and encourage more flowers. Taller plants will need staking to protect them from wind and rain, but the shorter varieties are perhaps more resistant to damage from foul weather than any other annual. Marigolds appreciate adequate water, but don't overdo it. They easily rot in soggy soil. In short, don't pamper these plants. They are rugged and tough and require only the minimum of attention. Marigolds will self-sow profusely, and the new progeny will be full of surprises, as this plant is variable from seed. (This is especially true of hybrids.)

Thunbergia alata

(Black-Eyed Susan Vine; Clock Vine) HH.

Uses: Screen, ground cover, hanging baskets, containers, vine to grow up netting, fences, trellises, lampposts, and other supports.
Color: Orange-yellow, yellow, white, most with dark centers.
Height: 6 feet, occasionally higher.
How to Start: Sow outside after final frost, or indoors 6 to 8 weeks ahead. 70–75°, 10–15 days.
Where to Plant: Prefers rich,

moist, well-drained soil high in organic matter. Sun or light shade. Regions with cool summers are best. Avoid reflected heat.
Spacing: 12 to 18 inches.
Care: Water well. Avoid pruning this plant.
Native to: Tropical Africa.
There is an exotic crispness to the flowers of this vine, with their overlapping yellow or orange petals and startling black eye. And the light green, ivy-like leaves provide an appropriate background. The common name is a bit misleading, as the blossoms don't even remotely resemble the daisy-like flowers of the prairie "black-eyed Susan."
This tropical vine climbs by twining stems. If you grow it on smooth columns, lampposts, or against a wall, be sure to provide something for it to grab onto. Like many vines, it is equally attractive spilling down from walls, steep banks, or from hanging pots. Thunbergia is particularly suited to growing in portable containers, which allow bringing it in for winter color. Plant it outside the following year as soon as the spring heats up, and you will be amazed at its increased vigor in the second year of growth.
Yellow and orange types with or without the black eye are the most commonly available. A pure white form, both with and without the black eye, is more rare.

Tithonia rotundifolia

(Mexican Sunflower) HH.

Uses: Background, screen, rear of border, cut flowers.
Color: Reddish-orange.
Height: 4 to 6 feet.
How to Start: Sow outside in place after last frost, or indoors 6 to 8 weeks ahead. Cover seeds only lightly, as light may assist germination. Constant 70°, 7–21 days.
Where to Plant: Prefers average, well-drained loam. Tolerates heat and drought.
Spacing: 2 feet.
Care: Easy. May require staking, especially late in the season. If flowers are used for cutting, sear the hollow stems to lengthen life. Do not overwater.
Native to: Mexico and Central America.
The Mexican sunflower is one of the largest plants grown as an annual. Huge, coarse leaves 6 to 12 inches long clothe shrubby, erect stems that may reach 8 feet high, although 4 to 6 feet is the rule. In mid-July the plant begins producing brilliant, fiery red-orange flowers with yellow centers. They resemble large single dahlias and are borne at the ends of many branched stems. The color is so rich and intense that it takes only a few flowers to create a strong effect. Its size and coarse texture limit its use to the background in the border. Few annuals suit this function, so the rust-resistant Mexican sunflower fills an important gap.
Be sure to stake them to prevent breakage in strong

wind. The flowers are choice for cutting, as long as you sear the ends of their hollow stems.

Torenia Fournieri

(Wishbone Flower) T.

Uses: Bedding, edging, containers, hanging baskets, indoor plant.
Color: Combinations of violet, purple, yellow, and white, all in the same flower. New varieties are tinged with pink or red.
Height: 8 to 12 inches.
How to Start: Sow indoors 10 to 12 weeks before the final frost. Do not cover the seeds, as light is needed for germination. 70–75°, 15–20 days.
Where to Plant: Fertile, moist, fluffy soil high in organic matter. Partial to deep shade. Appreciates high humidity. Indoors, give indirect light and a night temperature of 60°, with indirect light.
Spacing: 6 to 8 inches.
Care: Keep well watered. Before first frost in the fall, dig, pot, and bring inside for winter color.
Native to: South Vietnam.
Quiet and unassuming, the wishbone flower is a little-known gem that should be a favorite of the discerning shade gardener. The individual flowers are especially interesting viewed up close: their structure is similar to the snapdragon, to which they are related, but the coloring is more reminiscent of the pansy. The

Tithonia rotundifolia

Thunbergia alata

upper petal is a pale blue, the lower lip a deep violet, and the center is yellow. Two yellow stamens arch over the center in the shape of a wishbone, from which the plant receives its common name.

Touch the center pistil of torenia lightly and an interesting phenomenon occurs: the two lobes of either side of the flower gradually close to hold tight any pollen that might have dropped.

In the garden the plant forms a loose clump covered with tiny flowers. It is not a flashy flower by any means, and prefers a cool, damp retreat in a shady corner. Flowers fade quickly in bright sun and dry climates. Planted either in large beds as a ground cover, or dabbed here and there, the deep, cool colors with a slight yellow sparkle are particularly appropriate in dappled shade.

Trachymene coerulea

(Blue Lace Flower) HH. Formerly known as *Didiscus caerulus.*

Uses: Beds, borders, cut flowers.
Color: Pale blue.
Height: 24 to 30 inches.
How to Start: Best to sow outdoors in place after final frost, as this plant transplants with difficulty. If started indoors, do so 6 to 8 weeks ahead. Constant 70°, 14–21 days.
Where to Plant: Best in light, sharply drained, sandy soil with plenty of organic matter. Prefers regions of cool summers. Does not tolerate heat well.

Spacing: 12 inches.
Care: Water only moderately. May require staking.
Native to: Australia.

The blue lace flower is a recent introduction to American gardening that is still relatively unknown. Feathery, grayish leaves cloak tall, delicate, hairy stems that in July and August are topped with powdery blue umbels strikingly similar to Queen Anne's lace. The flowers, on curving stems, are a treasure for arrangements, to which they lend an airy delicacy.

Standing alone in the garden they appear quite forlorn, and their hairy foliage seems to act as a magnet for dust. This is a plant that needs company, and it blends well into the mixed border.

Tropaeolum majus
(Nasturtium) H.

Uses: Trellis, screen, beds, walls, hanging baskets, window boxes and planters.
Color: Yellow, orange, red, white; some bicolored.
Height: 12 inches, some trailing up to 10 feet.
How to Start: Easiest and best to sow outdoors in place after final frost. Germinates in 7 to 14 days at 65°.
Where to Plant: Best in sandy, dry, infertile but well-drained soil. If soil is too rich there will be much foliage and few flowers. Best in regions of dry, cool summers. Tolerates drought.
Spacing: 8 to 12 inches.

Care: Easy. Do not fertilize. Water well.
Native to: The Andes in South America.

Too often experienced gardeners look down their noses and tut-tut the nasturtium as "too easy—mere child's play." This is unfortunate, for the gay, bright colors are nothing to sniff at (although some varieties *are* fragrant), nor is this vigorous, trailing vine that easy to grow *well.* Indeed, nasturtiums thrive in the poorest soils and require little care if grown in the right spot; but the gardener must be careful to give them plenty of moisture without overwatering, and avoid feeding with high-nitrogen fertilizer, which produces all leaves and no flowers. (The foliage is beautiful, and great to spark up a salad with its peppery flavor, but you'll get enough leaves for all the salads you could desire, without fertilizer.)

Give nasturtiums the coolest spot in the garden. Native to the high, moist slopes of the Andes from Peru to Colombia, they do not take well to excessive heat, faring best in regions of cool summers and high humidity.

Many colors and bicolors are available, and these named hybrids are far superior to the usual orange type. Some are dense, compact, bushy plants, growing only 12 inches high and maybe twice as wide. Some are semi-trailing types, and will creep around in a 2- to 6-foot circle. Others are trailing plants or weak climbers that may reach 6 to 10 feet in length. All nasturtiums need special support by tying in order to climb, as they lack any

Tropaeolum majus
'Whirly Bird Rose'

Tropaeolum majus

Trachymene coerulea

Torenia Fournieri

appendages for grasping, and do not truly twine, but rather twist and snake about.

Trailing nasturtiums are excellent in large hanging baskets, and the compact varieties in large pots on the patio. Plant them in beds all to themselves, train them up trellises, or erect supports.

Verbena × hybrida
(Garden Verbena) HH.

Uses: Ground cover, beds, rock gardens, walls, containers.
Color: Bright blues, red, white, pink, purple, lavender, yellow. Often with a white eye.
Height: 6 to 8 inches.
How to Start: Sow seed indoors 12 to 14 weeks prior to final frost. The fine seed is sensitive to dampness, so water minimally and do not cover the seed with soil. Seeds do, however, require darkness for germination. The best technique is to moisten soil 24 hours in advance, plant the seed, then keep the flats or pots wrapped in black plastic until they germinate. 70–75°, 3–4 weeks.
Where to Plant: Prefers well-drained sandy soil of high fertility. Full sun. Good air circulation. Quite tolerant of heat, but may temporarily cease flowering during intense hot spells. Moderately tolerant of drought.
Spacing: 12 to 18 inches.
Care: Water only moderately. Prone to mildew in heavy soil and damp locations. Fertilize heavily and regularly.
Native to: Of hybrid origin. Parents native to subtropical

and tropical South America.

The riotous color of verbena is one of the easiest ways to brighten hot, dry spots in the garden. Few annuals can match its intensity of color. The plants are generally low and trailing with deep green or grayish, aromatic foliage. They are excellent as edging, in solid, brilliant beds all to themselves, or in window boxes and planters.

Verbena will not flower well in shade, and in damp, stale air they are likely to mildew unto death. When planting in containers, give them a mix of equal parts of compost (or peat), loam, and sand.

Some flowers may be pleasantly scented, although this is rare among today's hybrids. At one time essence of verbena was an important perfume commercially and the plants were noted for their fragrance. The modern hybrids, while infinitely more colorful, have, sadly, lost their original scent.

Viola × wittrockiana
(Pansy; Viola) Perennial grown as a hardy annual. Highly cold-resistant.

Uses: Bedding, edging, rock gardens, containers, cut flowers.
Color: White, purple, yellow, red, pink, orange, bronze; some in combinations.
Height: 4 to 9 inches.
How to Start: The object is to have strong plants in early spring so that you can have bloom before summer heat

sends them into decline or kills them. Most gardeners rely on bedding plants from the nursery, but in mild climates you can sow directly outdoors in late summer or winter. Elsewhere, pansies are most often sown in late summer and grown over winter in a cold frame. However, you can sow indoors 6 to 8 weeks prior to setting out in early spring. Darkness is required for germination. Sow seeds in a moist flat, chill in the refrigerator for 4 or 5 days, then keep the germinating medium in darkness at 65–70° until they sprout, in 10 to 20 days. Then grow the seedlings in a cool, 50° environment.
Where to Plant: Rich, moist, well-drained soil high in organic matter. Prefers full sun, but partial shade satisfactory. Does not tolerate heat. Best in cool-summer regions.
Spacing: 4 to 6 inches.
Care: Mulch soil to keep roots cool. Fertilize regularly; keep well watered. Remove faded flowers to prolong bloom. Choose heat-resistant varieties.
Native to: Of hybrid origin. Parents native to Europe and possibly Asia Minor.

It is difficult to believe that these large, brightly colored hybrids are descendants of the quiet, diminutive woodland violets. Like their parents, pansies are actually perennial, and in mild, cool climates the foliage will remain evergreen. But pansies are almost universally treated as annuals, and short-season ones at that. Heat destroys them, and in all but the coolest climates the long-

est season you can hope for is from May to July. Heat-resistant varieties have been developed for longer bloom, but even they need the care cited above.

Pansies provide brilliant color and are often used around the perimeter of beds of late-blooming bulbs. They also can make adequate beds themselves, but it is difficult to plant them closely enough to cover the ground before the heat takes them. It is wise when you plant pansies to always have in mind a successive planting of a late-blooming annual.

Zinnia elegans
(Common Zinnia) HH.
Zinnia Haageana
(Mexican Zinnia) HH.
Zinnia angustifolia HH.

Uses: Bedding, borders, edging, containers, cut flowers.
Color: Flowers are single or double. Zinnia elegans comes in all colors except blue. Z. Haageana has single or double flowers in red, bronze, orange, or yellow bicolors. Z. angustifolia has single, small flowers in faintly striped orange and yellow.
Height: Z. elegans, 6 to 40 inches; Z. Haageana, 12 to 18 inches; Z. angustifolia, 12 inches.
How to Start: Easy to sow directly outside after final frost, or sow indoors 4 weeks ahead. Lightly cover seed. Double-flowered varieties can temporarily revert to single flowers when transplanted, and can

Verbena × hybrida

Viola × wittrockiana

suffer from shock; so it is best to start these outside where they are to grow. 70–75°, 5–7 days.

Where to Plant: Fertile, well-drained soil rich in organic matter. Best in hot, dry climates with long summers. Full sun. Good air circulation.

Spacing: 6 to 12 inches.

Care: Easy to grow, but mildew can be a severe problem. Never water late in the day, and avoid getting moisture on the foliage. Best to soak or flood when watering, but be sure to water regularly. Use fungicide if mildew appears. Fertilize regularly. Pinching young plants will result in denser foliage, more blooms. Remove spent blossoms.

Native to: Mexico.

Plant breeders have had a field day with the zinnia, and the continuing results have placed this plant near the top of the American popularity list. A profusion of forms and heights means that there is a zinnia for nearly any garden purpose. They are available in an almost limitless range of bright, festive colors, often in brilliant mixes. The long-lasting blossoms, borne on tall, strong stems well covered with foliage, are ideal for cutting.

It seems curious that this complex, varied plant symbolized simplicity in Victorian times, yet simplicity aptly describes the older, pure species of zinnia, of which limited supplies are still available to the contemporary gardener.

Zinnia angustifolia (formerly *Zinnia linearis*) is a pleasant ground-cover species whose spreading, prostrate form and lush dark green foliage carry flowers all summer long.

Zinnia Haageana, the Mexican zinnia, grows a little taller, with blooms that are similar but which can be single or double.

When most people hear the word zinnia, they think of the fluffy, double flowers of *Zinnia elegans*. The hundreds of its cultivars are usually grouped into three categories according to size: dwarf, intermediate, and tall. But the lines are not distinct, and much intergrading often confuses the issue. Within each category many strains of flower form and size have been developed, in nearly every color of the rainbow. The dwarf and intermediate varieties are excellent for bedding or containers, as they flower abundantly and often spread quite wide. Use the taller varieties in the mixed border toward the rear, and in the cutting garden, where any necessary staking will be least noticeable.

Zinnia flowers are long-lasting in arrangements, but be sure to choose buds that are just starting to open and cut them early in the day. Experienced growers of cut flowers look for the long-stemmed varieties with rather small dahlia- or beehive-shape flowers on graceful, curving stems. Giant-flowered types have massive blossoms that work best in large arrangements.

The secret to growing good zinnias is to keep the foliage dry. Give them plenty of heat and air circulation, and avoid cool locations of damp, stagnant air.

***Zinnia elegans* 'Fruit Bowl Mix'**

Zinnia angustifolia